C000050369

POOR MAN, RICH MAN

The priorities of Jesus and the agenda of the church

POOR MAN, RICH MAN

The priorities of Jesus and the agenda of the church

Peter Lee

HODDER AND STOUGHTON
LONDON SYDNEY AUCKLAND TORONTO

British Library Cataloguing in Publication Data

Lee, Peter, *1944–*
    Poor man, rich man: the priorities of
    Jesus and the agenda of the church.—
    (Hodder Christian paperbacks)
    1. Clergy—Office
    I. Title
    262'.14   BV660.2

ISBN 0 340 39305 X

Copyright © 1986 by Peter Lee. First printed 1986. All rights reserved. No part of this publication may be reproduced or transmitted in any form or by any means, electronic or mechanical, including photocopy, recording, or any information storage and retrieval system, without permission in writing from the publisher. Printed in Great Britain for Hodder and Stoughton Limited, Mill Road, Dunton Green, Sevenoaks, Kent by Cox & Wyman Ltd, Reading, Berks. Typeset by Hewer Text Composition Services, Edinburgh.

Hodder and Stoughton Editorial Office: 47 Bedford Square, London WC1B 3DP.

For the poor

CONTENTS

FOREWORD

Most bishops make a point of exhorting their clergy to cultivate habits of reading and study to enrich their ministries and be able to keep abreast of developments in their particular sphere of activity. Sadly this exhortation has suffered the fate of many another well-meant piece of advice – that it has made little impact on the lives of those for whom it was intended. One of the first things that has impressed me about Peter Lee's book is the evidence it provides of one priest who has heeded the admonitions of his bishop. Peter Lee has read widely and to good effect. He has clearly read, marked, learned and inwardly digested and we have benefited from his conscientiousness.

The second noteworthy fact is that Peter, coming from a so-called evangelical background, has not permitted himself to be hamstrung by the usual evangelical parameters that have tended to confine salvation to a pietistic and individual concern for single souls and their relationship with their God. It is refreshing, especially in the South African context, to have a white evangelist who realises that the gospel of Jesus Christ is a whole gospel for the whole person and that it does not tolerate false dichotomies between the secular and the sacred, between politics and religion, between contemplation and action. For that I want to thank God fervently because it is getting boring for some of us constantly to assert that a biblical and incarnational faith cannot tolerate any area of life in which God's writ does not run.

What is even more impressive for some of us is to have someone in the renewal movement in South Africa, and one who is white to boot, who has not given the suspicion that involvement in the so-called charismatic movement has been a respectable cop-out. People for whom I have a great deal of time such as Bishop Bruce Evans of Port Elizabeth, one who is involved in the same movement as Peter, has told me that most of the 'white' parishes in our Anglican church that have shown any significant concern in the harsh socio-political and economic issues of South Africa have been 'renewed' parishes. That assertion Peter repeats. I can certainly attest to the fact that his parish, St Luke's, Orchards, – thoroughly 'renewed' – is reflected in his book as the parish that goes to black resettlement camps, helps to build schools and churches and sleeps on dirt floors among the uprooted and dumped blacks. I would hope this could be universally so. I don't think it is yet.

Peter speaks from a wide experience and his characterisation is sensitive and accurate. We have met at least some of those who people his book.

His criticism levelled against liberation theology is largely fair, though its exponents might say that at its best it considers the most profound liberation to be from sin – of which political oppression and exploitation are manifestations – and that liberation is in order for us to be all that God intended us to be personally and corporately.

I have found his discussion of the 'poor' most helpful and containing many insights we need to bear in mind if we are not to be too naive in our pronouncements. I am relieved that he recognises that the God of the Bible is not neutral.

This is a most worthwhile book which I commend very enthusiastically. I am proud that Peter is a priest in my diocese and I know we will hear a great deal of this outstanding person. God be praised.

† DESMOND, JOHANNESBURG

PREFACE

This book is about the ministry of Jesus, the mission he gave to his church, and the restoration of his workers to the wholeness of the work he has for them to do. It is less an academic treatise than a hasty despatch from the battlefront. It has been written in the gaps of an averagely busy parish ministry, and I hope that what it has thereby lost in theological precision or stylistic consistency it may gain in immediacy. I identify with William Barclay's self description as 'a theological middleman'. The pace of publishing and the rapid change taking place in South Africa may make the illustrations *passé* by the time they appear; I hope the principles can be reapplied.

There is no resemblance between either the characters or the churches caricatured here and any real ones alive or dead. They are constructs from many pieces. I am not rector of St Agnes' – though as it happens, I was of Alexandra. It may be helpful to read in conjunction with this volume my forthcoming book which is a survey of the South African situation to be published in 1986.

Thanks at this point are due in four directions. First there are those who have made the book possible in practice: Michael Green, who has been an inspiration for many years and who opened up the possibility of this volume on a dirt road somewhere between Johannesburg and the Botswana border en route for a clergy conference together in 1983; Mrs Jenny Thomson, who typed a good chunk of the book; and the folk at Hodder and Stoughton, notably David Wavre.

Second there are those who enabled me to live, to live

11

Christianly, and to pursue the Lord's priorities as I see them in my own ministry: Gill and the girls, who have tolerated what the French call an *auteur dissipé* – that is, distracted or absent-minded – around the house; our church's supportive pastoral team and all the brothers and sisters at St Luke's, Orchards, St Michael's, Alexandra, the Parish of the Good Shepherd at Tladi in Soweto and all around the place – all of whose love, encouragement and perception help to keep my perspectives right.

Most difficult to pin down is my theological debt, owed as it is not only to remembered books, events and teachers, but to that whole absorbed environment of faith and learning which comes from prayer and study, discipleship and exposure to people over time. My debt to Leon Morris' Commentary on Luke (New International Greek Testament Commentary, Paternoster 1978) will be obvious. I am grateful not only to theologians but to those Christians who practise their faith in face of the world and whose activity leaves as much a challenge as the writing and speaking of others.

Finally I must thank my bishop and South Africa's second Nobel Peace Prize winner, Desmond Mpilo Tutu, for graciously writing a foreword.

PETER LEE, 1985
Biblical quotations are from the New International Version

1 AGENDA NEEDED

Dorcas Selele is blind, black and old. She lives in Alexandra Township, a single square mile of residential chaos on the opposite corner of Johannesburg from the massive sprawl of Soweto. Widowed these twenty years, since a mining disease took off her husband, she lives with teenage daughter, her son and daughter-in-law, their two sons, her married daughter and son-in-law, three of *their* children, two young cousins, a dog, three chickens and a goat in their four-roomed house in 13th Avenue. (There was a cow until the children laughed at Dorcas for not being detribalised.) They are lucky to have one of the old brick houses, some ten metres square, which can stand a corrugated-iron lean-to on two sides and a make-shift room of heavy plastic sheeting behind one of those.

Life is not bad for Dorcas; true, there are neither drains nor street lights in Alex, and in six months in 1981 there were 165 murders, 118 reported rapes and 600 reported assaults in the overcrowded mile; this past Christmas people bled to death in the passage at the clinic because the doctors couldn't sew any faster. But she is with her family and they care for her; the house may be crowded but the children go to school, two of the men and her daughter-in-law are at work and her grandson, Zipho, will soon complete his B. Comm. and earn good money. Their joint income is adequate if they share it. She has friends all around, sings twice a week with the Mothers' Union in praise of her God, and can sit in her full and active church (rickety though the building is) in the front pew on the left where the disabled who can't walk up for communion gather together.

Dorcas' lot, of course, needs improving. They have solved the queueing for pensions, but not for the clinic; her income is mean, her home over-full and the township itself poor and dangerous. Yet in terms of her quality of life, her past joys and present relationships, she is surprisingly slow to complain.

Dorcas' sister dreads next week in Soweto, where the pension queues have not yet been solved. The system seems efficient enough; you go every second month to whichever of the eleven pension points is yours, and – provided your papers are in order – you get the money. At Emily's point there will be 3,000 women in the queue (the men collect the next day), so it takes time. They begin to gather in the early hours, and by 7 a.m. – when a church from the 'white' northern suburbs, working with a team from her sister church in Soweto, begin distributing soup, bread and a smile down the line – the majority will be there. The queue is in the open, so heat is a problem in summer and cold (at 2,000 metres above sea level) in winter. One of the winter workers said the queue seemed to thaw as the soup and the love went down the line. The money arrives after nine, and the disabled – who come by taxi, walking stick or wheelbarrow – go first. The Salvation Army captain will bring a wheelchair for the disabled and a megaphone to greet the people, lead some singing and preach. The pension itself, graded down by law according to race, will go to basic necessities; whether it covers them depends on how meagrely you can live.[1]

The church of Jesus Christ, meanwhile, is under orders to serve the myriad Emilys and Dorcas Seleles of the world, and to preach good news to them. But what, in their setting, does that mean? In their case, where do the Christians begin – with preaching, provisions or protest? With their immediate bodily needs, their social deprivation, their pensions or their souls? If Jesus came to Alex, where would he start with Dorcas?

Alice Barrington is well off. When the divorce went

through eight years ago she got the house – five bedrooms, a swimming pool and the rest – on a half acre in what the *Guardian* calls 'some of the most opulent suburbs in the world', halfway from central Johannesburg to Alexandra. Her maintenance lets her keep on the gardener and two domestics (all black, of course, and one of them Dorcas' daughter-in-law); although the pay is only average – perhaps twice an old age pension, or a little bit more – they are glad to have it. The worst part of the job is Alice's endless complaining, for few other ears will now bother to listen. Her bridge circle meets every week, and two of her children dutifully bring their families for lunch once a month (sorting out 'duty Sundays' by phone behind her back). The other son, Simon, went off the rails and she chooses not to speak or hear of him – getting first into grass, motorcycles and parties, then (worse) into left-wing politics, and then (worse again) catching 'born-again' religion and going to teach in a Soweto high school. Her decent son is at least a managing director and her daughter landed a lawyer so, if they can avoid divorce in a city where half the marriages go that way, she can at least take pride in, if not love from, her grandchildren.

As for daily life, she rises late (why not?), has a drink or two with lunch and some more as the day goes on; it helps her sleep, and if she becomes part of the 6% of South Africa's white population who are alcoholic (and who buy half the liquor industry's annual turnover), what is that to her? No one pays her any attention any more, not even the church; she once had links with two local churches, but one went political in 1976 and the other doesn't care about the old: the minister took to sending a lay woman to see her instead of coming himself, and that wasn't what she paid her dues for.

The Christian church is called to love, serve and preach good news to Alice. But what, for her, is that? A pastoral pat on the head from her minister might keep her happy, but not set her free; faithful Christian friends might support her but not evangelise her; and Amos-like denunciation of her affluent and exploitative lifestyle might be fair but ineffectual – still less charitable. For she is, as it happens, dying of cancer, and she is human too . . .

Solly Menachemson leaves school next year – a daunting prospect, as his parents, second-generation immigrants, put him into one of the rapidly flourishing, expensive and exclusively Jewish schools in Johannesburg. His folk are among the 60,000 or so Jews in the city's half-million strong white population, a group whose social and economic impact is strongly felt (and quite widely resented). They have stimulated the economy, brought in skill and energy, and plunged into philanthropy; formed a high-profile bloc of Jewishness with synagogues, special schools, a rabbinic academy and an intensely 'us and them' mentality.

Solly feels the threat because as yet there is no Jewish university, and the thought of either army service, university or work in a multi-cultural setting makes him anxious. He can only feel the half-belonging identity that his grandparents felt in Poland; no piece of ground, not even Israel, feels like home to him or his people.

For all that, the Christians are largely to blame, taking the long view. Nonetheless they are called today to care for this pale and lanky adolescent, and to bring him news that will make for his peace. But what form must it take, and how can it be done?

Fanie's Afrikaans blood boils when Solly, or Alice, or Dorcas present themselves at his Post Office counter. This has been his people's land for generations; they prayed for it, fought for it, wrangled for it and got it. But he has had none of Solly's privileges, only two years' army (a privilege, but no fun) and then stuck behind a counter in a half-protected government job. It pays badly and sniffy types looking for packets addressed to English names like Barrington are all he needs; they seem to have it all, and he resents them. Then come the Seleles, wanting to mail things to places he has never heard of and doesn't want to, always bringing the wrong money and not writing straight or knowing what to ask for. At least before the queues were integrated you had some days without them, and you didn't have to mind what you said to them; now there's always some troublemaker writing to the manager. Fanie wouldn't mind so much if he could afford to live in this part of town, but the wife and kids are in a poky place in a run-down suburb and have no hope of moving out of it. Funny promised land for the Afrikaners to be fighting for – and if they open his job to the blacks,[2] what then? Work alongside them or starve is a poor prospect. And as for *under* them . . .

In a land where so many churches have fought bitter battles, and so many conflicting causes claim the name Christian, the followers of Jesus still have to address themselves to Fanie van Vuuren. But what is the good news for him? What are its cost and its implications? Is it essentially a challenge to his politics, his personal attitudes, his religious assumptions or his patriotism? Christians don't agree; nor do their synods, theologians or spokesmen. If they did, they might win a hearing.

Simon Barrington's muddy Volkswagen stands at the roadblock. The police want to know where he and Zipho are going. Yes, they accept that he has a permit to travel in Soweto to his school. But what is he doing with a black in his car? They are much of an age; do they think they are being clever? Zipho is a student, is he? And what does he belong to – ANC, Azapo,[3] anything else?

It hits Simon hard. Not until late teenage was he revolted by his parents' treatment of blacks, and then he was too busy indulging himself at their expense to get involved in change. But the drug scene is quite political and as he was drawn to the one he was exposed to the other. That blew the fuse at home, when his friends horrified his father and his views his mother. If anything, his Christian conversion had alienated Alice even more, if that were possible, though oddly it was a logical step from both the church education they had bought him and from the angry politics of the left. Political friends had seemed so right in their passionate fury at apartheid and their willingness for sacrifice to change it; by contrast the churches seemed so soft, so collaborative. But there was a gap, a hardness against conciliation, a running out of compassion, a need for ultimate vindication in a worldview beyond that of socialism or Marxism, yet more selfless and highminded than materialistic capitalism. Both his mind and his heart had led him to Christ, to drink from a source of both forgiveness and freshness that satisfied mind and ideology as much as heart and spirit. The plunge into Soweto was somehow both smaller and more specific, if less grandiose and deeper in personal cost and daily tedium, than the sloganising of the politicals. It somehow seemed the Jesus place to be, despite the ordinariness of it and its criticism as compromise by radical friends.

Zipho Selele had been a serendipity. Although travelling the other way religiously – from genuine inherited faith towards cynicism under the impact of the fading credibility of the church – he could sense a kindred spirit when he met one. Simon was to him a straight, open, struggling spirit trying to be himself with compassion in a messy society. He seemed befriendable. He was neither superior nor somehow out to curry favour with the underdog. And Zipho could simply accept him and like him as a friend.

In any other country it would have been a natural, easy contact between open hearts, university minds and kindred spirits. They could debate the need for change, the place of violence in reaching it, the relevance of Christianity, economics, law, justice and the basis for racial relations in a divided society. Here, it was under pressure. Looks from pedestrians, sniping from Simon's staffroom colleagues, Zipho's rejection by hardline radicals for associating with whites – and now the roadblock. Would they have taken the seat out and checked so carefully with another passenger? The entire apparatus of South African disapproval settled dreadlike on their minds as they drove on, wondering how to say that they wanted to go on hanging around together.

In our part of town, the churches are active; most denominations can afford to build, and run a busy programme. Alex too is religious – over 100 churches, groups and sects are at work in that one square mile. Yet oddly enough, neither Dorcas nor Alice, Fanie nor Solly would feel at home in more than one or two of them, and not the same ones at that – so much have culture, language, race and history captured the one universal church of Christ.

Take St Agnes' Anglican. In its lovely post-Gothic building, well-groomed friends of Alice Barrington find a pew week by week (or at least once a month) by the stained-glass window in memory of the fallen in the Anglo-Boer War (the Anglo fallen, that is). The rolling phrases of the rich old Prayer Book arouse nostalgia and some spirituality, while immunising the hearers from a good deal else. The fête goes well, for the people have money and need a new roof for the lych gate; they care for the poor and send food now and then, though they jump if the bishops make political statements (these churchmen aren't in touch with reality). True, there are one or two parish ladies in the Black Sash[4] and the church has just produced its first conscientious objector to military service; but things are fairly quiet really and they still pray in church for 'the boys on the border', trying hard to forget the kitchen maid's son who fled the country after the '76 riots and is also on the border in another way. While Alice feels it is too political, Simon wishes it would go much further in both social relevance and spiritual vitality: it all seems so complacent, so slow, so out of touch. They will innovate here and there in the parish but draw the line at anything too holy, too spiritual, too political, too charismatic, too anything . . .

Bridleway Bible Baptist is refreshingly focused by contrast. It 'knows the gospel' and the minister preaches it weekly – to teach the believers on Sunday morning and win the unsaved in the evening. After all Jesus said he had come to preach good news and that is what they are doing. They send out missionaries, their youngsters go to Bible college, those who don't head for the mission field can be elders at Bridleway Baptist while they are succeeding at business in town. There's a care for the poor (though one mustn't discourage people learning to work for themselves) and blankets are given at Christmas to the Bible school students in Soweto. They evangelise in Alexandra (Mrs Selele's still an Anglican despite all the tracts) and do their best to teach the truth amid the error in the cults. At a certain point in his discipleship, Simon had been greatly helped by Bridleway – but somehow he seemed to outgrow it.

Corybantic Charismatic Chapel proves very popular. Since the local Methodist minister was filled with the Spirit and seceded he has had a tremendous following in the school hall, where people speak in tongues and are healed every week, and so many people come to Christ who had sat in churches for years without being blessed. It's amazing how different it is, really working in the Spirit . . . people are coming in who have been turned off by all the politics in the mainline churches and are just seeking the Lord, praise God. Some pray every day for the nation to be redeemed and all the people to come to a saving knowledge of the Lord. There's been a suggestion of getting involved with the needs of the hungry, and there was a funny word of prophecy a couple of weeks back which said much the same; maybe the Spirit is trying to say something, but his ideas go beyond our assumptions . . .

The Dutch Reformed keeps off politics, for although there is ferment among the theologians and trouble with the World Alliance of Reformed Churches, the elders don't stand any nonsense. The dominee[5] thanks God weekly for his gift of the land and the Afrikaner's trustee role in it. When Fanie van Vuuren does his next army camp (he does them gladly, he knows Romans 13) they may make him a deacon and let him carry the plate. They care about the blacks God has put in their charge; they are even allowed to have their service every Sunday afternoon[6] in the garage by the church hall. The elders let them have the minister from the daughter church in the township to come and preach (though there was a bit of a rumpus when the dominee wanted him to preach to the whites in the church). Each year on 16 December there is a lovely service of thanksgiving for the victory when God gave the land to their ancestors and so many Zulus were killed. Thank God he is with us and we don't have politics in our religion . . .

Emmanuel Presbyterian is political. It has a very committed minister who says God loves the poor and wants the structures changed and hadn't we noticed the parable of the good Samaritan was about race relations? The congregation is now multiracial and some people have left and it's a nuisance having some of the prayers in Xhosa and the sermon translated every week as the preacher goes along; but there's a warmth and a care, and sharing the peace at communion is quite an experience. Simon and Zipho have attended together, without the discomfort they would feel anywhere else. But the spiritual ones say Jesus hasn't been mentioned since Christmas and they wish the minister would stop lashing the government, after all they are in a very difficult position . . .

Such illustrations of human need and of the churches' response could be multiplied with different local colour in every country in the world. True, the South African colours are vivid, which makes it a good place to grapple with the issues – at least one can see them clearly. South Africa has the distinction of holding in itself the same racial proportions, numerically speaking, as the world; and it has the First World-Third World economic relationship which characterises the world as a whole within its boundaries. It also conveniently represents the theological spectrum in its multifarious churches. But the needs and the debate are universal – and that is what this book is about. Perhaps it can be summed up in two questions. When Jesus said, 'The Spirit of the Lord is on me, because he has anointed me to preach good news to the poor',[7]

– What did he mean for himself?
– And what are the implications for his church?

Those, in various forms, are the most vexed and vital questions facing the Christian church in the remainder of this twentieth century.

We begin with these words of Jesus because they are pivotal in two ways. Biblically speaking, they are represented by Luke the evangelist as the blueprint for Jesus' ministry, the way to his self-understanding and his vision of the work in which he was about to engage. It is clearly critical for the church to understand what its founder thought he was doing.

Further, if this very same commission is explicitly transferred to the shoulders of the church by its Lord, it becomes essential for today's Christians to have a precise notion of what that commission is. It is for this reason, speaking contemporarily, that these words of Jesus have come to stand at the crossroads of our life in the church. They form a point of departure for the life and thinking of several utterly different Christian groups. It is almost as if today's church has these words of Jesus 'on the brain' like a well-known song – they crop up so frequently in such contrasting places. When the same phrases are quoted or alluded to in the Lausanne Covenant, in the personal prayer letter of David du Plessis (known affectionately worldwide as 'Mr Pentecost'), and in the sermons and statements of Bishop Desmond Tutu, something is up. This, I believe, is because these words of Jesus bring together three of the greatest preoccupations of today's church – the power of God's Spirit, the content of his message to the world, and the crying needs of the poor.

It would be wrong to caricature at this point, but at least in terms of emphasis it would be true to say that the Pentecostal churches and charismatic Christians in other churches would read these words one way, evangelicals would read them another, and adherents of liberation theology would read them another. It is true that there are many in the churches who would not sit under any of these banners, and also that few Christian leaders could be neatly boxed into any of them; true too that much cross-fertilising of theologies has gone on in recent years and that many charismatics, evangelicals and liberationists would increasingly acknowledge not only their theological debt to each other but also that their goals and attempts at mission 'touch sides' with each other more than they either did or believed they did in the past. It is critical that each Christian and every school of thought in the church confirm and share what is true in his view of things, to allow what is disproportionate to be corrected, and to move towards that precise and whole vision which is grounded in the example and teaching of Jesus.

That, then, is the aim of this book – to look again at the work and words of Jesus to try to grasp what his own priorities in ministry were; and then to see what that says to the church in its pursuit of its agenda today. We will do it by trying, initially, to unpack the priorities of Jesus in four ways: first by taking a spanner to Luke 4, dismantling his own statement of aims carefully and seeing what it consists of; second, by reviewing widely the Old Testament material which we can reasonably believe was in his mind when he cited it in the Nazareth synagogue announcement; third, by looking at what he actually did with that statement of aims when it came to his ministry itself, seeing what sort of ministry he offered to whom and why; then looking at the teaching he gave in passing, for the light it sheds on his programme. Most of this will be based on Luke's gospel, with sideways glimpses of the others. Then we may be able to assess the relevance of all this to the church, both original, perpetual, and contemporary, and to the inhabitants of the world nearby.

2 PRIORITIES STATED

The Spirit of the Lord is on me,
    because he has anointed me to preach good news to the
    poor.
He has sent me to proclaim freedom for the prisoners
    and recovery of sight for the blind,
    to release the oppressed,
    to proclaim the year of the Lord's favour.[1]

Those rolling, thrilling, shattering lines – for us as for his
hearers – are given us by Luke as Jesus' own announcement
of his programme. They had more than once formed the raw
material of debate in Simon and Zipho's developing friendship. If Jesus still had any relevance to us, Zipho argued, it
had to have something to do with the poor as we know them.
Simon, in his new-forged Christian experience, was more
sure that Jesus was relevant but less clear about how – and
where the poor fitted in, though his heart was sure that they
did. Can we still get back to what Jesus intended them to
understand?

The nativity accounts in Luke 1 and 2, which form a
section by themselves, are behind us (on their significance,
see p. 88). So is the beginning of John the Baptist's ministry.
Jesus has been baptised by John and the Holy Spirit has
come upon him in that event. The same Spirit has led Jesus
into the desert for a time of prayer and preparation for
ministry in which the devil has also come to test him. Jesus
has then moved into Galilee – 'in the power of the Spirit' –
and begun to act in such a way that 'news about him spread

through the whole countryside'.[2] His action included his teaching, for 'He taught in their synagogues, and everyone praised him.'[3] The proclamation, whatever its content, was clearly a main cause of the news which, even in days of slow travel, could spread round the modest area of the Galilee fairly rapidly. But something more than teaching was going on, as Jesus hints in Luke 4:23, where it is clear that he has already been in Capernaum – a larger and more strategic centre than Nazareth. He has there performed powerful works of some kind, for he caught the Nazarenes saying, 'Do here what you did there!'

Luke continues:

> He went to Nazareth, where he had been brought up, and on the Sabbath day he went into the synagogue, as was his custom. And he stood up to read. The scroll of the prophet Isaiah was handed to him. Unrolling it, he found the place where it is written:
> 'The Spirit of the Lord is on me, because he has anointed me to preach good news to the poor. He has sent me to proclaim freedom for the prisoners and recovery of sight for the blind, to release the oppressed, to proclaim the year of the Lord's favour.'
> Then he rolled up the scroll, gave it back to the attendant and sat down. The eyes of everyone in the synagogue were fastened on him, and he said to them, 'Today this scripture is fulfilled in your hearing.'[4]

Luke is the only evangelist who records this passage so fully, though Mark and Matthew report a similar order of events for the beginning of Jesus' ministry with differing emphases (see Appendix I). We need to ask ourselves what caused Luke to record this particular passage and to give it such prominence as a kind of headline for what follows – in the gospel and in Acts.

Luke notes that Jesus went on the sabbath day to the

synagogue 'as was his custom'.[5] This is deliberate. Luke is often described as writing to a largely Roman readership (whoever Theophilus was[6]) and attempting to portray Jesus and the early church as essentially safe, loyal citizens – certainly no threat to Rome as the Jews might try to present them.[7] Certainly, in the process, Luke both records and implies criticism of the Jewish leadership. On the other hand, it is not often enough said that Luke is just as concerned to emphasise the loyalty of Jesus and his followers to Jewish teaching and tradition.[8] Jesus may have assailed the Jewish establishment – though Luke plays down the accounts compared with Matthew – but on routine matters he honoured the traditions, the places of worship, and the Jewish law. When conflicts do arise he is seen, as in Matthew, not opposing the old Jewish way with radical innovation, but more normally attacking current traditions in the name of a principle which may look new but usually rests on an abiding Old Testament basis with a fresh cutting edge in Jesus himself. So here Luke takes one opportunity to stress the habitual nature of Jesus' attendance, and quite possibly the fact that it was, by now, his habit to *teach* in the synagogue wherever he could.[9] None of this, of course, could soften the dramatic content of this particular teaching when it came.

What happened next is not clear. It would be usual for set readings to be followed, and the reader would be given the scroll open at the right place. It seems that Jesus was routinely given Isaiah, rather than choosing it, but that he then deliberately unrolled it and 'found the place'.[10] Having read an unusually short section,[11] which he deliberately cut in mid-sentence, he sat down in the usual manner of a Jewish teacher[12] and began to comment on the reading. This would be the right of any responsible adult male allowed to read in the synagogue. Luke's record of his comments, 'Today this scripture is fulfilled in your hearing,'[13] may be a summary of extended teaching or may record precisely what Jesus said, as surprising in its brevity as in its bluntness.

The reading from Isaiah

The passage Jesus chose is quite crucial for our understanding of his ministry, and of what Luke means to emphasise; so are a number of critical details.

In the first place, the passage from Isaiah 61 is traditionally reckoned among the 'servant songs' which come in the later section of Isaiah (chs 40–66). In these chapters both the immediate restoration and the long-term blessing and liberation of Israel are prophesied and celebrated. Within the extended promises come several pictures of a figure, God's supreme servant, who will be used to bring these ends about. At some points it appears that the servant is the prophet himself; at others it seems to be Israel as a whole. Yet beyond these nearer meanings, a figure stands out to whom the Jews could look forward, a self-giving yet triumphant person who would outstrip all their heroes, kings and deliverers to date. It is this fact which gives these chapters their eschatological flavour, that is, their sense that God's ultimate purpose and rescue are in view beyond Israel's pressing historical circumstances. This being so, the figure of the servant inevitably attracted messianic overtones as the agent of that purpose.

The servant songs themselves are passages in which the Lord is heard speaking of the servant and his role and authority, or in which the servant himself is pictured responding to the Lord and to his own God-given role. The 'songs' are normally demarcated as Isaiah 42:1–4; 49:1–7; 50:4–9, and 52:13–53:12. The passage which Jesus quoted at Nazareth, Isaiah 61:1–4, is thought by some to contain the Israelite community's first reflection and commentary on the songs, but the exact literary relationship and origin in Israel are virtually impossible to tie down precisely (see Appendix II). The effect is clear, that in Judaism there was an expectation that God would send a servant to rescue his people through suffering and that he would send one or more mightily anointed prophets to announce his word. From other strands of the Old Testament there were expectations of a kingly figure who was also anointed as God's envoy or Messiah, and many Jews quite probably saw that figure as mirrored in the Isaiah promises too. It was therefore not surprising that in common parlance, or in apocalyptic fantasies of God's victorious future, these hoped-for figures became confused or conflated in people's minds.

Qumran is important here. In this long-lost ascetic community by the Dead Sea, apocalyptic expectations were treasured and enshrined in the books of the community, which were kept alongside commentaries on several books of the scriptures. The community has to be dated not far from Jesus' day and affinities are often adduced between it and John the Baptist. The place of Isaiah 61 in contemporary thinking is highlighted by the fact that it is used of the Teacher of Righteousness – the leader and a teacher of the Qumran community[14] – and quoted in the Melchizedek document.[15] The latter passage ties Isaiah 61 itself firmly into the servant thinking of Isaiah as a whole, not only linking it with Isaiah 52:7 – 'How beautiful on the mountains are the feet of those who bring good news, who proclaim peace, who bring good tidings, who proclaim salvation, who say to Zion, "Your God reigns!"' – but stressing that it is God's servant *anointed by the Spirit* who will do the bringing of the good news. Referring to the end of days, the passage identifies 'he that bringeth good tidings' as 'that is the anointed by the Spirit, from whom He says . . . and that which He says: He that bringeth good tidings of good, that publisheth salvation: that is which is written concerning him, that He says . . . to comfort . . .'[16] Even in this fragmentary form of the passage the connection is clear. It is striking, in view of what Jesus goes on to say in the synagogue, that this same passage links the day of jubilee with God's release of the nation from exile in Babylon.[17]

The role of the Spirit of God in the Old Testament is largely anonymous, but two things about his role are clear. He came upon individual leaders, and especially God's spokesmen such as the prophets, to teach them, deepen their communication of God, and empower them to communicate God's word and purpose and power to men. He was also envisaged as coming in some later day upon all men – at least upon all Israel and quite possibly a wider community of faith – to enable them from within their beings to fulfil that righteous style of life which the Old Testament community found notoriously elusive and difficult. In seizing upon Isaiah 61 and declaring that it was now fulfilled in their hearing, that is in himself, the very least that Jesus was claiming was that the long-lapsed authority of the Old Testament prophets was now revived and resting upon himself. That claim is reinforced in his words about Elijah and Elisha while still in the synagogue.[18] Thus while Jesus' words are not by themselves a messianic claim, they are but a short step from it. As Howard Marshall puts it, 'In Lk. the point is not the identification of the speaker as a messianic figure, but rather that the functions of this OT figure are now fulfilled in Jesus who has been anointed with the Spirit for this purpose.'[19] Granted the Jewish style of speaking in dynamic and functional rather than static or ontological terms, if Jesus is claiming to *do* whatever the figure in Isaiah was to do, he was not far from claiming to *be* whatever Isaiah intended by his words.

We should now look more closely at some details in wording in Luke 4:18–19. Several of these arise because of the difficulty in knowing where Jesus' wording (or Luke's account of it) came from. Most of the Old Testament was, of course, first written in Hebrew, and was then translated into a Greek version (the Septuagint, normally abbreviated as LXX) over a period from the third century BC to the second century AD. Most of the New Testament citations of the Old Testament are either directly from the LXX or are loose versions of it derived from memory (as today a preacher may loosely conflate the King James and other versions in a passing reference) or from being translated back from Aramaic (the language Jesus and his followers almost certainly spoke, with perhaps some Greek). The quotation with which we are concerned[20] shows a number of variations on the LXX which may well be deliberate and will, in that case, be significant.

The central claim

Before we dive into such details, we can set down the central thrust of what Jesus is saying.

In the first place, the Spirit of God is upon him. The punctuation (which is not, of course, given in the Greek New Testament) should probably be 'The Spirit of the Lord is on me, because he has anointed me. He has sent me to proclaim good news to the poor, to announce freedom . . . etc.'

This being so, his confidence in the fact that he bears the Spirit is rooted in a definite experience of the coming, the anointing with that Spirit. This is then a reference to his baptism.[21] Although the gospel accounts vary, the central elements of Jesus' baptism seem to be:

1. A washing with water which identified him with the others who were coming to John in repentance, though he is not seen as needing to repent of sin himself.
2. A coming of the Spirit in birdlike form, which he knew about and the onlookers may have.
3. A confirming word from heaven, that is from God the Father, which is drawn from two or three Old Testament passages suggesting sacrificial, messianic and 'divine servant' roles for Jesus.[22] Thus the 'servant' theme in Isaiah 61/Luke 4:18 has been adumbrated already from Isaiah 42:1/Luke 3:22.

Jesus, then, is claiming that the empowering of God's Spirit, which not only came upon certain Old Testament heroes and spokesmen but was envisaged for a (then) future figure outstripping their stature, has taken place for him. He *is* the person, *has had* the experience, and *now has* both the commission and the power and authority to fulfil it. The word 'experience' may jar with some in these days when 'spiritual experiences' are all the rage for some and highly suspect with others who want to stand only on 'objective truth'. But experience it was, and inspiring, motivating experience at that: without it no such claims as these, and probably no such ministry as followed, could be envisaged. The most reductionist account of Jesus' baptism that we can give is that the evangelists (if not Jesus) record Jesus (if not the onlookers) as having a visionary and auditory (if not visible or audible) experience which, by their own later account, both motivated and directed what followed in his life and work. That is an experience, and if its fruits are anything to go by, we could do with more people having more like it.

He is, then, equipped by the Spirit for a purpose: 'He has anointed me to preach good news to the poor.' Here the Spirit, who is later (especially in Acts) the Spirit of Jesus who equips and sends Jesus' followers, equips Jesus himself. This is wholly in line with the expectation set up in Luke 1 and 2. 'Sent' is the word behind 'apostle' or 'apostolic'; it means 'sent out, despatched, thrust off'; a forceful term, and one which implies an authority of the sender over the sent as well as an empowering of the sent by the sender.

'To preach good news' is a single word, literally 'to evangelise' – or more purposively, 'that I might evangelise'. The word has, for us, somewhat limiting connotations from modern evangelism, but is the Bible's common term for announcing or heralding good news. The LXX uses it in Isaiah 52:7, 'How beautiful on the mountains are the feet of those who evangelise'. So Paul writes, 'Timothy has evangelised us of your faith' (1 Thessalonians 3:6), and the angel tells the shepherds 'I have come to evangelise you of a great joy' (Luke 2:10). We should not, therefore, limit too quickly the meaning of this 'good news' which Jesus is to announce to the poor. It will be qualified in following verses and more fully in his ministry and teaching as a whole. We are wise not to read back our own preconceptions, whether of spiritual salvation or social liberation, into this very general headline phrase.

The object of his preaching will be 'the poor'. Here again we are faced with a basket expression which needs careful explaining and qualifying, and we are wise to reserve judgement for a while. It is far too easy to say, 'Because it says "the poor" it means the poor as we see them on twentieth-century TV screens.' It is also too easy to say, 'Because he is talking of preaching good news it must mean the unevangelised.' We need to know what was in the mind of Luke, or, if we can, of Jesus. That is not so elusive as it may appear. Since their minds were fed from the Old Testament, its usage will be essential if not decisive (see chapter three). And because we have an account of some years of Jesus' activity and a good deal of teaching attributed to him, we can grasp some idea of those to whom he thought his news was addressed (see chapter four).

For the present let it be said in summary that the term 'the poor' hints at a group of Old Testament words which cover every kind of deprivation – material, judicial, emotional and spiritual – and that there is a strong suggestion that these are the '*godly* poor'. That is, one can say correctly that the Old Testament shows a God especially concerned for the poor; but that is not to express the whole truth. The God of the Bible looks for those who honour him, and the poor he seeks are those who seek him. 'The poor' and 'the poor in spirit' are not as far apart as may appear.

The details

We now need to turn to the details in Luke 4:18–19. We call them that deliberately, for if the punctuation we have adopted is correct, then all that follows is an explanation of what we have so far – that is, 'to preach good news to the poor' is not the first of five activities to which Jesus is called; it is rather the headline announcing the whole of his calling, of which the remaining four phrases are an enlargement and explanation.

The missing 'broken hearted'. Some ancient texts of Luke, though not on the whole the most reliable of them, insert 'to bind up the broken hearted', a phrase which has otherwise dropped out of Isaiah 61 in the LXX in Jesus' quotation. Again it is not clear whether Jesus (or Luke) is just quoting loosely, or whether (as is possible) the phrase stood in Luke's original and has been lost in some texts en route to us, or whether there is some deeper significance in its omission. This last is quite unlikely, as the two themes of the phrase – healing and the people who have been crushed by life – are covered in the later phrases and would not be in evident conflict with any of them. It is worth noting that there is no way in which the term can be 'stuffed' into either a liberationist or an exclusively spiritual interpretation of Jesus without strain and artificiality; Dorcas and Alice both qualify.

Freedom for the prisoners. Three Greek words must be weighed here. We have seen how New Testament quotations of Old Testament passages sometimes vary in wording, and here is a case in point. The first word, 'to proclaim or announce' has shifted from a general word in LXX meaning 'to call out or say publicly' (*kalesai*) to a term with much more specific Christian connotations, 'to herald' (*kēruxai*). There may be no significance in the shift, but the latter term which now stands in the text did become one of the characteristic terms for preaching in the specific sense of proclaiming the Christian message. This may, therefore, be a piece of loose memorising by the writer, or the understandable tendency of language in the Luke who had himself preached and been in close company with others, notably Paul, who were heralds of the gospel and used this vocabulary.[23] But it may have been Jesus' own word, with whatever application. In any case, we note the main point that Jesus did not claim to be about releasing prisoners as such, but about *announcing* their release. One may ask, as we look further at Jesus' own ministry, 'What prisoners did he in fact release in his lifetime and what kind of prisoners?' In the literal sense he only dealt with two that we know of, namely John the Baptist whom he encouraged (and thus released?) but did not free; and Barabbas, whom he only freed in an indirect, though deeply symbolic and theological sense.

This deep and theological sense is hinted at in the second word, 'freedom' or 'release'. While the word itself (*aphesin*), has a general reference, it is regularly used in the spiritual sense of *forgiveness*, i.e., release from sin and its consequences.[24] While it would be too dogmatic to exclude a wider or more practical reference here, it would also beg the issue to confine it to those in literal prisons.

The term for the prisoners (*aichmalōtois*) tends to refer specifically to prisoners of war, though not exclusively – Paul uses it of Andronicus and Junias, Aristarchus and Epaphras, all of whom had simply been imprisoned with him at various times and on the various charges brought against the apostle.[25] Since the nature of the release is not specific, the nature of the imprisonment should not be prejudged either.

Sight for the blind. Here we have just two words in Greek. The term for the blind is the common and natural one (*tuphlois*) for those who cannot see, but the usage of that word is again rather slippery. The idea is used in the Old Testament (especially in Isaiah) of the *spiritually* blind,[26] that is of those who either failed or refused to perceive the truth of God, or to take it seriously, or to follow it in their lives. Similarly in the New Testament Jesus is presented as healing several physically blind individuals, but in no single case does it stop there. It is always said or strongly implied that the effect of their new sight is that the healed see Jesus, and in seeing him see the point of his message, so that they admire him, or defend him from criticism, or follow him thereafter. There is thus a subtlety and breadth in the idea which should not escape us. Digressing for a second to our own day, we could say that there is an element of embarrassment here for more than one of the main schools of thought in its narrow form. The evangelicals get their emphasis on 'seeing the gospel' but have to contend also with the fact of miraculous physical healing. The liberationists have real trouble in giving 'the blind' a parallel content with their interpretation of the terms 'poor', 'imprisoned' or 'oppressed'. If they apply it to the blindness of the oppressor they are not always keen for new sight to bring healing; judgement can become obsessive. Alice and Dorcas *both* need help.

As for the giving of sight (*anablepsin*), this merely underlines the ambivalence in the blindness. In Luke 7:22 Jesus sends word to John the Baptist that 'the blind receive sight', which must have a literal meaning as well as any deeper one; yet another of Isaiah's servant songs sets the same idea in a wide context of God's covenant blessings.[27]

Release for the oppressed. Here the English conceals three Greek words, literally 'to send away the broken in release'. This is an insertion from Isaiah 58:6, either added by Jesus while reading (an odd but not – for him – impossible procedure), or later in explanation by Luke or earlier storytellers on whom he drew. The term for 'release' is the same as for the prisoners above, so again carries the Christian doctrinal implications of forgiveness as well as the literal ones. 'To send away' is simple but potent, implying the joyful explosion into freedom of those who have been unable to enjoy free movement, liberty, energy or sunshine. It echoes the exuberance of the song of Moses in Exodus 15, which all the people sang as God – far more than Pharaoh – sent away the oppressed out of bondage in Egypt.

The key word here is 'the oppressed' which has such emotive and specific overtones in today's English. Its form is a passive participle of a verb meaning 'crush, bruise, or break'. Thus it means those who have suffered the crushing effects of the actions of others, or of life itself: that is, it could as easily mean someone heartbroken through adverse circumstance, as someone actively suppressed or enslaved by another human being or by unjust law or evil social structure. That last meaning is specifically included, however, for it occurs in the often-cited passage from Isaiah 58 (not a servant song, but not far from that context) in which the nature of true fasting – and thus of authentic religion – is outlined:

> Is not this the kind of fasting I have chosen:
> to loose the chains of injustice and untie the cords of the
> yoke,
> to set *the oppressed* free and break every yoke?
> Is it not to share your food with the hungry and to provide
> the poor wanderer with shelter –
> when you see the naked, to clothe him, and not to turn
> away
> from your own flesh and blood?[28]

The social, economic and political implications are here unavoidable: Dorcas won't go away.

At this point we should remind ourselves that Jesus was not alone in the synagogue. He was surrounded by Nazarene hearers, who were – as a good mixture of religious, half-religious and non-religious Jewish villagers – mentally reacting as they listened. These were citizens of an occupied territory, who knew what it was to be crushed under the Roman boot. Whether they felt the heel of their Jewish leaders too is not clear, though several hints in the gospels suggest that Jesus' onslaught on the Jewish leaders' oppression of their own people earned a widespread 'hear hear'. Whether at a basic level of nationalistic anger or at the more erudite one where apocalyptic thinking and writing flourished, they were all fed with visions of liberty rooted in their Judaic faith and scriptures. It was, in other words, quite impossible for Jesus – had he wanted to – to use such language as this, from such a hope-filled section of scripture, without hooking into at least some of the political and nationalistic expectations of his contemporaries. Correct their perspective he might, but escape it – when using this kind of source material – he manifestly could not. The implications of this we need to examine in time.

The year of the Lord's favour. Looking for a second at the four words alone, we have here a repetition of the verb 'to herald' as with release for the captives; then an adjective and noun, 'the acceptable year' or 'year of favour', and the uncomplicated 'of the Lord'. The adjective 'acceptable' is not easy because in English it suggests that somehow man finds God's year acceptable. The meaning is rather the reverse, that it is a year *upon which* the Lord's favour rests, and thus a year *through which* his favour rests on his people. The two nearest uses in the New Testament are Luke 2:14, with which translators have also battled, where the angels announce, 'Glory to God in the highest, and on earth peace to men *on whom his favour rests*', and Luke 4:24, when Jesus says 'no prophet is *accepted* in his home town'. In both cases it is not the character of the recipient – men on earth, or prophets – which is in view, but whether or not the givers of approval – God, or the hometown – are willing to accord it. Thus Jesus refers to some kind of year on which the Lord sovereignly imprints his special favour, or love, or approval, or blessing.

This phrase is almost certainly an allusion to the year of jubilee decreed in Leviticus 25, about which a mighty literature has developed in recent years. Whether or not such a year was ever implemented in Israel, the intention of it is clear enough. Israel, being uniquely a theocracy – a society ruled by God – had to reflect in its social conduct, as well as its worship and morality, the standards and character of its Lord. At the same time, provision was made for men to acknowledge God's rule and to reflect upon, and adjust themselves to, his teaching. Thus the sabbath, a weekly day of rest and worship, was not merely a convenience but an integral part of life. Busy men laid aside work to worship, pray, and hear the law; to readjust, in other words, to God after the distractions of working life. Trust in God was renewed by evidencing the belief that one did not need to work all day and every day, but could trust God enough to do it his way and know he would keep things going on that day, for it was he who kept everything going. The annual festivals, which also had specific purposes of remembrance, harvest thanksgiving, and so forth, rested on the same thinking regarding the sabbath principle. The principle has been well expressed in recent years by Rabbi Joshua O. Haberman of the Washington Hebrew Congregation: 'On the Sabbath I must acknowledge God as Creator by resting from my acquisitiveness, because I have no real title to anything. The Sabbath is the day that fully shows God as Creator. In it we add nothing to what he has done. For the first time in history the Sabbath brought a cessation from human acquisitiveness.'

Something similar happened – or was decreed to happen – on an annual basis. Every seventh year[29] the fields were to be left fallow, the farmers were to rest, and the hand of God would be seen providing adequately for society through self-seeding crops and unpruned vines and trees. This was, of course, wise agricultural practice in such a society, but it is reductionist to see it as that alone, religiously enforced. There was a theological principle too, that the whole experience would renew the people's trust in God's provision, giving the people recreation and an opportunity for study, worship and reflection. A sorting out of all kinds of matters should result, as fuller exposure to the Torah led to abandoning idolatry and worshipping the Lord, to the correction of personal moral matters, and to the reordering of any social affairs or relationships which had become unjust with the passage of time. Little of this is explicit in the Old Testament, but all of it is implicit in the obedience expected of the people, and in the use to which the sabbath – and sabbath year – was always expected to be put.

The year of jubilee was the pinnacle of all this. After seven sets of seven years – and thus after the forty-ninth year, the seventh 'fallow year' – came the year of jubilee once every half-century. In it the same provisions applied as in the seventh year, namely no planting nor organised harvesting beyond the needs of subsistence. But it went further, effectively achieving a 'back to square one' effect in terms of land and slavery.

'Square one', in this case, was the initial land allocation by tribes after the occupation of the land of Joshua's time. The basic principle here – and very fundamental it is – was that no land could be held either freehold or in perpetuity. The principle is in Leviticus 25:23 (God speaking): 'The land must not be sold permanently, because *the land is mine* and you are but aliens and my tenants.' This is basic. As in so much of Africa, and as the colonising powers so rarely understood, the only landholding system was usufruct and not by freehold ownership: that is, one could have – or buy, sell, or exchange – the right to *use* the land, but not the outright perpetual ownership of it. This arose from a basic understanding of the nature of God, and led to a clear and specific set of understandings where economic relations and social justice were concerned. The aim, and the effect, were to outlaw the material aggrandisement of the individual to the point where the poor or the less fortunate could never recover their position or share in opportunity.

The guarantee of this was the year of jubilee in which three main lines of action were intended:

1. The land was to lie fallow and unworked.
2. Each family was to return to its ancestral lands, which were effectively redistributed – not equally, but on the basis of original clan landholdings of Joshua's time.
3. Slaves (who could only be non-Israelites) were to be released, and Israelites who had had to become hired workers (and would otherwise have been slaves) were also to be freed from any further obligation.

What this amounts to is a deliberately planned and divinely commanded social revolution every half-century. Accumulated wealth was largely redistributed, accumulated disadvantage (especially selling oneself into bondage through indigence) was cancelled, and everyone went back to the economic starting line. It sounds unjust at first hearing, but was in fact carefully orchestrated. For example, land sales at any point depended on the time still to run before jubilee – 'because what he is really selling you is the number of crops'.[30] It was no disincentive to effort or industry, because the jubilees were well spaced. If jubilee fell early in a man's life, he had all the rest of it to work at. If it were late, he had had his good time. If in the middle, he had already had a good slice, and had plenty of time to start again. Looked at from the other side, of the lazy or the unfortunate, the advantages stand out clearly. Every man had a species of equal opportunity. If he fell into debt or difficulty, there was always hope somewhere ahead – and if he were frankly a wastrel, at least his family could not suffer the price of it through the next generation. In perhaps a rough-and-ready way, yet with more justice and more sophistication than most other societies have ever achieved, it was a recipe for social justice. At the very best – and looking at today's most unjust societies, it was a major point – it prevented the kind of irreversible injustice by which the rich and powerful can entrench their privilege in law for generations, and others can be left hopeless, unfree, and without opportunity decade after decade. In a way it was the perfect combination of the socialist vision of just sharing, which often falls down on the lack of incentive to work, and the capitalist practicality over incentives, hard work and opportunity, which so often falls down equally on the tendency of the 'haves' to entrench injustice interminably. Being based too (through the reversion to ancestral landholdings) on that solid social structure which keeps much of the Third World viable, the mutually committed family, it offered a 'small is beautiful' alternative to the unwieldy, impersonal and bureaucratic side effects of both socialism and capitalism.

No one knows whether this grand vision ever happened.[31] Some would argue that AD 26–27 was to be a year of jubilee and might have been in some people's minds when Jesus preached. In a way this is immaterial, for the vision of justice embodied in the idea served as powerful fuel for people's longings, regardless of dates. For 'the year of the Lord's favour' was more than a fifty-year event, it was identified with the Old Testament's vision of the 'day of the Lord', that great day to which all Jews looked forward, when God would implement his kingship, crush his enemies (and theirs) and establish justice, joy and peace in Israel. While the views of that day ranged from the more religious to the more nationalistic, they all foresaw the day as a single and final event in which all the ideals of jubilee would not only be renewed for a few decades but fulfilled and transcended for ever.

It was, therefore, a mighty claim of Jesus when he asserted that he had come to inaugurate that very thing. If he had only claimed to care about the observance of the regular 'year of jubilee' he would have been building a very explicit commitment to social justice and human liberation into the blueprint of his ministry. If he was claiming, as his choice of Isaiah 61 suggests, to be bringing in the *ultimate* jubilee, then all the more is this true.

The vital full stop. It is often and rightly remarked that after speaking of the year of the Lord's favour, the most significant thing Jesus did was to stop. For Isaiah 61:2 says, '. . . to proclaim the year of the Lord's favour *and the day of vengeance of our God*'. Here the identification of the 'year of the Lord's favour' with 'the day of the Lord' is very crucial, for the latter was a day in which the Lord not only saved *but judged*. Indeed, much of the message of the prophet Amos lies in the fact that the Jews of his day were self-righteously anticipating the day of the Lord as a triumph for them over their foes, whereas he has to warn that anyone involved in sin or disobedience should rather dread that day because of the judgement it must entail:

> Woe to you who long for the day of the Lord!
> Why do you long for the day of the Lord?
> That day will be darkness, not light.
> It will be as though a man fled from a lion only to meet a bear, as though he entered his house and rested his hand on the wall only to have a snake bite him.
> Will not the day of the Lord be darkness, not light . . . ?
> But let justice roll on like a river, righteousness like a never-failing stream![32]

Assuming that such a crucial line would not be haphazardly omitted, we have to ask the significance of Jesus' omission. It can be seen, in fairly conventional terms, as Jesus' approach to eschatology (that is, to the way God plans to wind things up at the end of time). Jesus has neither instituted the Lord's

great day in all its fullness and finality (what some call
'realised eschatology'), for there is still a climax, a crisis, a
judgement ahead of mankind; nor has he merely added to the
line of prophets and teachers, for he has done that unique
thing, he has inaugurated the 'last days', the new age of
God's special blessings in his Son, even though there are yet
matters to be completed.

Another tack, which may complement this, is to say that
this is part of Jesus' critique of his hearers' militant
nationalism. They, like their forebears of Amos' day, maybe
saw the Lord's day of vengeance as primarily directed
against their national enemies rather than against all
godlessness, evil and disobedience. Therefore Jesus may well
have introduced his claims from Isaiah to draw attention to
his own person and role, but then omitted these words in
order to begin educating his hearers about the *kind* of divine
servant, Messiah, leader or saviour, he was setting out to be.
Such an understanding would be entirely in keeping with his
approach in other places, most obviously in the events at
Caesarea Philippi as recorded in Matthew and Mark as well
as Luke.[33] Here Jesus, having ministered publicly for a
while, asks the disciples to report on what the public
speculation is making of him, and then to give their own
views. He then – and only then, but immediately then –
'began to teach them that the Son of Man must suffer many
things and be rejected by the elders, chief priests and
teachers of the law, and that he must be killed and after three
days rise again'.[34] In other words, he gave them the evidence
with which to lead them on to the belief that he was 'the
Christ, the Son of the living God';[35] but then he immediately
began to reinterpret for them what kind of Christ he was to
be, and how he was to fulfil the Messiah's calling. Something
very similar may be happening here in Luke 4, and would
certainly – as we shall see – help to explain the anger and
rejection which followed in Nazareth. If he were speaking
into their nationalistic fervour, and denying its longing for

vengeance and refusing to be part of it, that would make
sense.

The sermon. Having stopped reading abruptly in mid-
sentence, Jesus handed back the scroll, deliberately under-
lining the point at which he had stopped: then in the manner
of the rabbi, he sat to teach. What follows seems clearer than
it is: '. . . he said to them, "Today this scripture is fulfilled
in your hearing."' As it stands, that is far too cryptic and
brief a sermon for the synagogue situation. What we have,
therefore, may be Luke's summary of an extended sermon
from Jesus: if only we had the rest! Alternatively, Jesus
may deliberately have spoken with shocking brevity, as if
once this were said there was little else to say, leaving his
hearers reeling as they faced the blunt question whether
to accept his claim or not. His words clearly electrified the
congregation.

The effect. With Luke 4:22 we run into considerable problems,
which again need careful thought. The NIV renders it, along
the line of most translations, as follows: 'All spoke well of him
and were amazed at the gracious words that came from his
lips. "Isn't this Joseph's son?" they asked.' The difficulty of
these words appears when set in context:

1. Jesus cites Isaiah 61.
2. He then, most provocatively, claims to fulfil it.
3. All spoke well of him and his gracious words.
4. They ask about his identity as Joseph's son, a question
   which – in the light of their approval – can only mean
   something banal like 'Hasn't our local boy done well?' or
   'Hasn't he grown since we saw him last?' – all fairly
   unconvincing.
5. Jesus then speaks (verse 23) of their reaction to him as if it
   has been really hostile – 'Physician, heal yourself! Do here
   in your home town what we have heard that you do in

Capernaum.' This is not in keeping at all with what has gone before.

6. Jesus expands this with a broadside (verses 24–27) on how home towns reject their prophets, and elaborates by showing how in the Old Testament God reached out through both Elijah and Elisha to the Gentiles – presumably because the reaction of their natural Jewish constituency was too obdurate and unresponsive to their message.

7. At this – presumably because of both his criticism of Nazareth and his anti-nationalistic allusions to the Gentiles – the people were furious and swept him out of town to fling him off the heights above the plain of Jezreel below, opposite the village of Nain (verses 28–29). Since this was both illegal and contrary to the sabbath it speaks of an overwhelming hostility.

8. Jesus 'walked right through the crowd and went on his way' (verse 20) – which, considering the way they took him to the precipice, most likely implies a miraculous deliverance of some kind, though this is not explicit. At the very least, the force of his character and the stature of his personality must have made some kind of outstanding impact to overcome the hostility of the people.

Given this, Jesus' blunt response to their approval and the apparently violent volte-face between verses 22 and 28 suggest that we may have been mistranslating verse 22. As it stands, it sticks out awkwardly in a passage which would be much more logical if it uniformly described hostility to what Jesus had said.

This is precisely what some scholars have recently argued. If one gives the words the neutral weight which they can carry, verse 22 can be translated like this: 'All spoke out about him (*martureo* means 'to bear witness', not necessarily with a value judgement as to approval or disapproval) and were amazed (*thaumatizo* records amazement without leaning towards either delight or horror) at the words of grace that came from his lips.' The term 'words of grace' (*logois tēs charitos*) is more precise than 'gracious words' and rightly focuses attention on the *content* rather than the *quality* of Jesus' words. Now it happens that the way Jesus has spoken would provoke just this reaction. To say he spoke gracious words is to beg the question of what they sounded like to his hearers. For some, his claim to fulfil Isaiah 61 would be far from gracious; it would rather appear shocking, prepos- terous, arrogant, blasphemous. And with the way in which he cut off the tail of his quotation, intentionally denying the vengeance so dear to his hearers' hearts, one would well imagine dire and livid indignation among his hearers, the more so according to the extent of their nationalism and zealotry.

It therefore seems wise to take verse 22 either in a neutral reading – 'All spoke out about him and wondered at the words of grace' – or even the equally possible negative sense which some scholars[36] advocate, i.e. 'they protested with one voice, and were shocked, because he only spoke about God's year of grace/mercy (and omitted the words about the messianic vengeance)'.

To reread the series of events above, substituting these words, is to make much more sense of the whole episode. The question about Joseph's son then has real weight: 'Isn't this the local boy? Who does he think he is (claiming to fulfil scripture)?' And especially, why would a Nazarene be so unpatriotic? Jesus would then be rightly responding to their hostility when he says, in effect, 'Next I suppose you will be challenging me to show you the miracles I have done elsewhere, since you anyway doubt my person and author- ity.' The blunt words about patronising home-town attitudes then make sense. Their attempted murder comes because, far from appeasing their indignation, he has further con- fronted their small-mindedness and unbelief and provoked their wrath to boiling point. He does, then, show them a miracle and heal himself from their murderous plans by escaping – the one sign they did not want to see.

The story so far. Jesus' words manifestly caused offence, and it was for one or more of three reasons.

One was personal. There is clearly a touch of the well-known phenomenon in life and literature, of the home-town resentment when the local lad who has made good appears to come back boasting that he is someone special. This is real and evident, but too trivial to account for the whole response.

The second was religious. As has long and traditionally been said, much of Jesus' life was made up of the reactions of Jewish people, leaders and traditions to a man who appeared to claim, both in word and implicitly, to be fulfilling strands of Old Testament expectation – especially when these were commonly held to be only fulfilled by the Messiah of God, and at the end of the age. For an ordinary man to pop up in the synagogue on a typical sabbath and claim to be fulfilling those things in the midst of life was too much. We need not quarrel with this traditional understanding; but if we accept it we must also accept the nature of the role Jesus was claiming to fulfil. As we have seen, it simply cannot be confined to a programme of social liberation without imposing limited and anachronistic meanings on the language. But similarly it is quite tendentious to exclude from his blueprint the concrete social implications of setting free the crushed or proclaiming jubilee.

The third was political. There may be a much more directly political strand in this passage than has been realised, because if Jesus is addressing the fierce nationalism of his contemporaries – still more, challenging its militancy – he was throwing down a very deliberate gauntlet. The physical violence he immediately suffered revealed just how near the surface of zealotry that reaction lay.

So far it seems that the target area of Jesus' ministry is a wide one, and its aims correspondingly broad. He feels for those who are trapped, both in spirit and in circumstance; for the physically handicapped as well as those who cannot see the truth, not least as it is expressed in himself; for the broken, bruised and grieving, whether their condition has been caused by accident or the malice of others; indeed for all those whose human experience is impoverished or deprived, whether medically, materially, emotionally or in the knowledge of God and his favour. To the whole range he promises to announce liberation and sight, restoration, hope and release. Yet in doing so he appears, with forethought and courage, to have blocked the way of violent partisan, racial or nationalistic action as the method appropriate to his ends. He has something to offer to Dorcas and Alice, Solly and Fanie, Simon and Zipho, yet something firm to say to each of them too. Exactly how he understood what he said and worked out its implications can be seen more fully if we look at both the Old Testament background to his Nazareth announcement, and the outworking of it in his ensuing ministry. We now turn to the first of these.

3 PRIORITIES PREFIGURED

As their debate went back and forth, influenced both by bits of the Bible which came to mind and by the daily experiences and encounters of their lives and families, Simon Barrington and Zipho Selele found themselves again and again at the same point. They needed to know what was in Jesus' mind. His words could be studied and yield more and more understanding, but somehow there was a whole world of assumptions which lay behind his every phrase, which only the history and teaching of Israel could illuminate.

It was Jesus the Jew who sat to teach in the synagogue. Its form of worship, the scroll in his hand, the debates about interpretation and fulfilment, all were familiar. The scriptures and their meaning framed his thought-world. His faith was in the God of Israel, creator of all, spiritual, mighty and moral. No man nor idol nor nation could supplant him, for he was God; yet he could be known as good, the God of love. It was from that love that man was made – to serve God and to rule his world, with feelings and wisdom and morals and love. Yet that man was invariably wayward – the scriptures were the tale of his wandering from truth in worship, in personal behaviour and social dealings. Idolatry, immorality and injustice were the sum of his sin. Yet God, unresigned to that waywardness, had chosen a nation through which to enact a plan of restoration for his world. Calling Abraham and Moses to found and establish the nation, he had liberated and planted his people Israel, giving them not only land but law – guidelines for worship and conduct, but also for the ordering of a society in terms of his will. The

Torah was never a burden but an outflow of God's mind, the expression of his purpose. It captured and embodied what he wanted. Even the ten commandments began not with obligation but with who God was and what he had done – 'I am the Lord your God, who brought you out of Egypt': now that Lord would enlarge the commandments into a code for the social life – reverence in worship, the sanctity of life, the centrality of faith, respect of persons, resistance to exploitation, compassion for the sick and needy. When the prophets later tore into injustice, they were not saying anything new – just pointing to the gulf between the status quo and the Sinai standard. But God was not only ruler and judge; as father and lover he set the pattern throughout Old Testament writing for both the worship and godliness of the people, and their human relationships of trust, love and care.

None of this happened automatically in Israel. God used the leadership of men – rulers, prophets, poets, priests and soldiers – to guide, exhort and challenge his people. What the post-Christian reader so easily overlooks is the intimacy with God which he permitted and encouraged in these men. It was not only the towering figures of Abraham and Moses but schemers like David, grumblers like Job or scaredy-cats like Jeremiah who experienced deep, continuing and natural relations with the Almighty. As these men well knew, it was not only their own day in which God was at work, but each of his interventions in Israel was a model, type or pattern for even greater things which he would do again. The Old Testament foresees a greater prophet than Moses or Elijah and a greater king than David. It sees a greater day of blessing and a fiercer time of judgement. It sees a greater exodus than from Egypt and a greater restoration than from Babylon. Wishful thinking it might be, but promise of God it might also be. If ever a people lived on hope, it was the Jews. And it was hope not only of national pride, nor even of individuals knowing God's salvation, but also of justice and peace, release and social harmony. It was good news for the poor.

Here we must grapple with exactly what the Old Testament meant by *the poor*. This is the crux of today's vexed theological issue, for the identity we postulate for the poor has a way of dictating what news we preach, or what slant of the news we emphasise. Dorcas is manifestly poor; is Alice? Wherein lies the poverty – emotional, cultural or spiritual – of Solly or Fanie? And are Simon and Zipho poorer or richer than they used to be, now that one is materially worse off and the other better?

In the Old Testament there are four Hebrew terms which most commonly express the idea, together with a couple of others which are used very little. They are far from clear cut, each bearing something of a range of meaning in differing contexts, all overlapping and shedding light on each other. They are:

ani (with *anaw*), meaning *humble, weak, lowly, meek, poor, afflicted*;

ebyon, meaning *desirous, needy, poor*, tending to emphasise *material* need;

dal, meaning *lean, poor, weak*;

rush, meaning *poor, impoverished* (a less common term).

By far the heaviest concentration of these terms occurs in only five books of very varied kinds, namely, Job, Psalms, Proverbs, Isaiah and Amos: but we need to be alive to teaching on the subject elsewhere, as we are concerned with the idea and the truth rather than the occurrence of vocabulary alone.

The poor in the law

Once we are alert to God's apparent bias towards the underdog, we notice that theme emerging early in the Bible. Genesis contains several examples of the normally hard-done-by younger (or youngest) brothers of families receiving exceptional favour (Abel, Jacob, Joseph), and that favour includes redressing the conventional imbalance of wealth. Abram the wanderer is the head of God's people. Ishmael, fruit of faithlessness and issue of a slave, is given a place in the promise. Joseph, the foreigner, the original of an Old Testament type (in Moses and Daniel) becomes prime minister of an empire – and then exercises his role for the benefit of the hungry, including non-Egyptians. So, while the underdog is not the central obsession he becomes in some modern theology – for that role is reserved for God, his love and his plan – the plan to bless the poor is clearly and quite naturally presented as the way God likes to work; 'he has scattered those who are proud . . . brought down rulers . . . lifted up the humble.'[1]

Exodus begins so powerfully on the same note that it has become a goldmine for liberation theology, and a type of much of its analysis of oppression as well as its protest writing. Certainly the scenario in Exodus 1, with its analysis of the rulers' paranoia at the rapidly-growing slave population and the growing oppression as they vainly try to contain it, has ugly twentieth-century parallels in every continent. God's early words to Moses in Exodus 3 appear at first sight to be a charter for the gospel of social liberation:

The Lord said, 'I have indeed seen the misery of my people in Egypt. I have heard them crying out because of their slave drivers, and I am concerned about their suffering. So I have come down to rescue them from the hand of the Egyptians and to bring them up out of that land into a good and spacious land, a land flowing with milk and honey – the home of the Canaanites, Hittites, Amorites, Perizzites, Hivites and Jebusites. And now the cry of the Israelites has reached me, and I have seen the way the Egyptians are oppressing them. So now, go. I am sending you to Pharaoh to bring my people the Israelites out of Egypt.'[2]

Such an interpretation, popular at Emmanuel Presbyterian, is valid enough but overlooks several other points. For example, God says 'I have . . . seen the misery of *my people*' (verse 7). The whole event only makes sense in the light of Genesis and of Abraham, i.e. of the choice and election of a specific people as the bearers of God's plan and promise. It is not a generalised offer of liberation to any people undergoing injury, though in an indirect way it embodies God's concern for them. 'I am concerned about their suffering' is the word of a God who is concerned about *suffering as such*; but it is because of the *special* role of Israel that God is *specially* aware of the misery of his chosen.

God also says, 'I have come down . . . to bring them up out of that land' (verse 8). True liberation theology deals with justice *within* a society, not flight from it: again the offer of 'a good and spacious land' is specific to God's plan for the world, not general to every situation of oppression. That way the result would be invasions and refugees, not liberation . . .

God also says he will 'bring them up . . . into . . . a land . . . the home of the Canaanites, Hittites, Amorites, Perizzites, Hivites and Jebusites'. But how did *they* feel about it? To use Exodus as a type of liberation theology is to overlook the fact that, *in the categories of liberation theology*, God is here promising to turn his people into far worse practitioners of injustice (including invasion, theft, pillage, and genocide) than were the Egyptians. This only makes sense in terms of a higher morality, the overriding need to establish a cradle for the birth of God's plan – and even then it needs some explanation. To misuse the exodus theme is to suffer the rebound.

God further says, 'the cry of the Israelites has reached me' (verse 9). Is this merely their cries of anguish, which he has already mentioned, or does he mean their cries – *to God for help*? The latter seems quite likely, and if so opens up a theme which will stay with us, that of the *godly poor*. Most of the Old Testament, without saying the poor are by definition godly (or God's), assumes that the poor will tend to trust God and emphasises that those among the poor for whom God has an ear most open are those who explicitly lean on him. This implied prayerfulness reinforces the thought that here we have *God's* people oppressed – not just oppressed people.

God specifically says to Moses himself, 'So now, go. I am sending you to Pharaoh . . .' (verse 10). As so often, the chosen people are headed by an elect individual, who is not only the spokesman for justice or for the people, but is supremely close to God and a spokesman for him. That is explicit in the remainder of Exodus 3, as Moses protests his inadequacy and is armed with the unanswerable commission, 'I AM has sent me' (verse 14). Here again it is a matter of being careful not to invent things: it is not true that anyone who speaks for justice is *ipso facto* either a man of God or his spokesman. Rather, God's leader will be *first* a man of God – available to his will; in the process of fulfilling that will, he is more than likely to protest injustice if he meets it. In a world where speaking politically has been equated with prophecy, the equation is too simple.

This being so, we see that the Exodus drama – which feeds into much of the New Testament's theology – tells us a good deal about the poor and oppressed, but we need to be careful to see exactly *what* it says. It is here that the chapters following the exodus itself form a useful corrective – the manna and the quail, the waters of Meribah – for a superficial reading would suggest that the liberated people should quickly settle into the blessed life of a just and unoppressed community. But here we see God at odds with the people and by no means blessing them automatically, for although they are his people they are unruly and far from godly. And it is their godliness, obedience and trust, not just their liberation, which is his concern. It is for this reason that much of the rest of the book of Exodus is devoted to provisions for worship, for the love of God is to be central to Israel's life.

What is not concerned with worship, is concerned with the ordering of a just and contented society. So we see Moses sitting as judge and needing to delegate that function because of the build up of the work – so early does a concern for doing right in men's many disputes raise its head.[3] We see him receiving the decalogue with its concerns for family stability, human life and sexuality, and the protection of property. And we see the beginnings of the detailed application of those principles in regard to relationships at work, slaves, social responsibility, debts, locking up criminals, and so forth.

Here the concern for the poor begins to break surface explicitly, and protection for all potentially exploited groups is quickly written into the basis of Israel's life. Masters are strictly limited in what they may demand of slaves or servants, how long they may hold them, and how they may punish them. When crime occurs, vindictive penalties are excluded in favour of the strict limit of 'eye for an eye', etc. Thus what is often cited as primitive in fact represents a huge advance – certainly over some of today's penal systems. All aliens – visitors, migrant labourers, immigrants or travellers – are to be accorded special respect. This group – even today the most quickly exploited in any society, from *The Grapes of Wrath* to *Cry, the Beloved Country* – are specially shielded, as their foreignness, lack of language and unfamiliarity with the culture render them peculiarly vulnerable to abuse.[4]

Widows and orphans are also vulnerable groups, as they were in New Testament times;[5] the more fortunate are to resist the temptation to take advantage of them.[6] The whole area of debt, too, with all the exploitation we know so well in interest rates, repossessions, and the rest, is strictly limited; a man's cloak cannot be pawned overnight lest he be cold.[7] The lawcourts are also controlled; the whole western tradition of judicial integrity rests on principles set out in Exodus. Witnesses are to tell the truth, and both they and the judge are to choose truth over popular pressure. False charges and bribes are out: redress at law should be in the reach of all, and not only of the wealthy.[8] Social security is also provided; the poor, who are more amply provided for in Deuteronomy, are already given a special place by being able to harvest where they will from the spontaneous growth of the Sabbath year.[9] Recreation, too, is built into the social fabric, and not for executives only, but for the shopfloor. No one has the right to require another to work on the sabbath.[10] There are the roots of today's best industrial legislation.

The main contribution of the book of Leviticus is the recording of the law of jubilee, which we have already examined in detail (pp. 38–43). It has a few further hints to offer, too. It is Leviticus which proceeds from the vital principle that all land belongs to God, to the conclusion that when he causes his land to bear fruit, it is not only for the landlord's profit: he means his poor, the widows, orphans and aliens, to be sustained from it. Hence the law of gleaning, by which corn was to be harvested with deliberate careless-ness, leaving the corners of fields and the accidental drop-pings for the poor to collect (they had to work for it too). Similarly, vines and olives were to be harvested only once, at the optimum moment, leaving all that ripened later for the needy.[11] The poor are meant to be fed from God's earth. It is Leviticus, too, in its detailed provision for sacrificial offerings and ceremonial cleansing, which introduces the principle that the poor in the land may be allowed to offer a reduced gift if they cannot afford the normal. This applies, for example, to the cleansing of lepers and of women after childbirth – this being the provision of which Joseph and Mary took advantage.[12]

The book of Numbers, being largely narrative, has no references to the poor in the few instructions it does contain. However, its one isolated use of one of the terms for the poor is of peculiar significance: 'Now Moses was a very humble (or meek, or poor) man, more humble than anyone else on the face of the earth.'[13] This well-known comment on Moses, which affords a backdrop to our understanding of New Testament meekness, points us in the direction of a vital fact.

In this context, where Aaron and Miriam are undermining Moses' leadership, there is no sense whatever in thinking that the adjective bears a material meaning. It can only refer to an inner attribute of character, something in the area of humility or unostentation or dependence on God. If anything it stands in contrast to the brassy attitude and language of Miriam and Aaron. Towards God Moses is submissive, towards himself modest, and towards others unassuming. The Torah here alerts us to the non-political content of the language of poverty which occurs often in the prophets and the writings.

In Deuteronomy, the most maturely codified area of the Torah/Law, comes an approach to the poor which is nearest in the Old Testament to lifting him above the level of an object of compassion into a well-nigh sacred figure; not in himself, but as the emblem of a society marked by God's own character of love and as the yardstick of its faithfulness. In legislating for the seventh year, the sabbath year in which debts are to be released, the law digresses to observe that with obedience in the land debt will barely occur, since God's blessing would be so rich as to obviate poverty – 'there should be no poor among you, for in the land the Lord your God is giving you to possess as your inheritance, he will richly bless you, if only you fully obey . . .'[14]

If a practical need does occur, God's first requirement is not action but attitude: 'If there is a poor man among your brothers . . . do not be hard-hearted or tight-fisted towards (him). Rather be open-handed and freely lend him whatever he needs.'[15] In particular, generosity is not to be held back by a swift calculation as to the unhappy proximity of the seventh year.[16] Generosity there is certainly to be, however: 'There will always be poor people in the land. Therefore I command you to be open-handed towards your brothers and towards the poor and needy in your land.'[17] This last overriding command (combining *ani* and *ebyon*) puts the words of Jesus in perspective, when he says 'The poor you will always have with you'.[18] His quotation of these words with the addition 'but you will not always have me' is not an egocentric dismissal of the poor but a reaffirmation of the law with due recognition of his own special place. His abbreviated reference was meant to put his hearers in mind of the whole and unaltered command. Unlike the false logic of modern fatalism which says 'There will always be the poor, so what's the point of trying?' the Torah's context of divine sovereignty and compassion insists on the reverse logic – 'Since they are always there and God always loves them, therefore we must always reflect his generosity and sensitivity to them.'

Deuteronomy goes further in urging a detailed sensitivity to the poor man's narrow margins of survival. A cloak may be taken in pledge for a debt, but if its owner is poor, must be returned for him to sleep in at night; and special arrangements must be made for wages to be paid daily since 'he is poor and is counting on it'.[19] Anyone who has worked where a flow of the destitute call for help 'until the end of the month' knows the merit of that instruction, at least until the industrious but unlucky have found their feet.

Apart from specific occurrences of the language of need, overall Deuteronomy is remarkably like the rest of the Torah with regard to all the things that matter to the underdog – restraint of arbitrary authority, respect for the courts, respect for the bodies of captive women or unprotected girls, places of safety to cool vendetta and allow due process of law; and even – *Laus Deo* – practical support for full-time religious workers.

The poor in the prophets

It is a commonplace of modern preaching that the towering giants of Israel's prophetic tradition were champions of the needy and scourges of the oppressive and careless. Before diving into the great written prophecies we should remind ourselves, first, that the entire pattern of Old Testament prophecy was set by Moses;[20] and secondly that the Jewish 'book of the prophets' includes not only the written deposits of the later prophets but the books from Joshua onwards which record the activity of the former prophets as well as – almost in passing, sometimes – the history of Israel.

Moses typifies the prophet in four key characteristics:

1. The prophet has *a special relationship with God*. Only God can call and appoint a prophet; from the prophet's viewpoint this tends to be recorded as an unexpected intervention in his life, an encounter with the Almighty which inaugurates a continuing relationship of exceptional openness and intimacy. For Moses this meant the meeting at the bush, the encounters at Sinai, and the continuing use of the 'tent of meeting' in which he repeatedly met Yahweh and was himself clothed in glory.[21] Part of this prophetic intimacy is a two-way communication in which the prophet receives his message to announce (often accompanied by insights into the future), and is also entitled and expected to intercede for the people and for their situations.

2. The prophet has *a special role in verbal proclamation*. This is not merely to predict, but rather to proclaim the words of God into both present and future with authority and knowledge. His message may be specific to the circumstance or an abiding principle. And as anointed by the Spirit, his voice has cutting power among his hearers.

3. The prophet has *a special place among God's people*. He is able to stir them from lethargy and give them a vision of what is going on around them, to change their perspective from everyday routine to know God among them in salvation-history. They acquire an historic role themselves in following the prophet's bidding (Moses and Egypt, Moses and Canaan). They are also to respond to his detailed instructions, for the prophet is also a lawgiver.

Torah is not a dull code by contrast with living prophecy; it is itself prophetic, a vision of a lifestyle set forth from the heart of God. This is not to say that the prophet is honoured in his lifetime; his very perception of the will of God and of the future sets him ahead of, and thus to a degree apart from the community. While they sit down he urges movement; while they rejoice he foretells tragedy; while they fear he is announcing restoration.

4. The prophet has *a special role towards the leaders of the community* whether they are part of the people of God (Moses to Aaron, Nathan to David, Amos to Amaziah), or outside the covenant people (Moses to Pharaoh, Amos to Edom). Because they stand for God's will and standards, they are champions of right and of justice,[22] and this brings them into constant conflict with vested interest. Moses was involved in his people's needs early on and continued to be so, both in Egypt, in the desert, and in planning for the promised land.[23] This ethical social commitment is a hallmark of true prophecy.

It is striking that the expectations of the Qumran community were that three great figures would appear in the end-time, the Davidic Messiah who would lead in military victory, an Aaronic priest who would be head of state, and the prophet like Moses who would announce to the people God's will for that era. Jesus spoke into a thought-world filled with notions like these.

If we look on to the 'former prophets', in the books of Joshua to Kings, we find that the term 'the poor' continues to include the unlikely lesser members of families or of the nation, upon whom God's election for leadership unexpectedly falls. So Gideon — one of those few on whom the Lord's Spirit is explicitly said to have fallen — is called to be God's champion even though he rightly protests, 'But Lord, how can I save Israel? My clan is the *weakest* in Manasseh, and I am the *least* in my family.'[24]

David, similarly, when anointed king as the least – and least likely – of the sons of Jesse, protests that he is 'only a poor man and little known'.[25] The long line of humanly unlikely choices for leadership in the Old Testament illustrates the same point: God chooses the poor, both to emphasise his capacity through grace to make them great, and because their simplicity often forms in them an openness to God which eludes the sophisticated and self-sufficient. Here we draw near to New Testament ground.

In the former prophets the poor continue, in practice, to be the objects of God's love and of the ministry of his servants. Jesus is only seizing on the most dramatic examples when he mentions Elijah's ministry to the Gentile widow of Sidon, and Elisha's to the Gentile general, Naaman of Syria.[26] Notice, incidentally, that the 'poverty' of these two is not only material but medical, and has also to do with the discovery of the true God of Israel – a 'spiritual' priority. The prophet Nathan represents the wronged Uriah,[27] Elijah brings life to the dead and speaks out for the dispossessed Naboth,[28] Elisha multiplies food in famine,[29] and so on.

God's defence of the poor and needy against improper use of authority is a recurring theme (Naboth again). In particular the king's role in expressing God's righteousness by implementing the law and upholding the rights of the needy is brought into sharp relief when Nathan turns the incident of Bathsheba against David.[30] David's initial indignant reaction to Uriah's story is wholly in keeping with the kingly role envisaged in the Psalms – and his repentance is precisely a recognition of how far he has abdicated his role and abused his power. David would wholly have endorsed the role of government portrayed in Romans 13:4, 'he is God's servant to do you (the people) good . . . an agent of wrath to bring punishment on the wrongdoer'. He is there to secure the Torah's principles, and to implement its protection of the weak.

This section of the Bible continues to emphasise poverty

as not only a material condition, but an emotional trauma, a social stigma, or a spiritual void. It is nowhere more eloquently put than in the 'pre-Magnificat' of Hannah,[31] the barren woman who has prayerfully sought and found a child. Her God 'raises the poor from the dust and lifts the needy from the ash heap; he seats them with princes, and has them inherit a throne of honour'.[32] She, too, has seen 'the consolation of Israel'.[33]

The sayings of the prophet Amos, identified as they are with the 'poor of the Lord' when he proclaims judgement all the way from his throne in Jerusalem to Mount Carmel in the north,[34] are of particular importance for us. It goes without saying that he is one of the prophets most burdened with the lot of the poor, the exploited, and the oppressed. Further, he stands at the head of the line of writing prophets, as if the corruption in Israel has provoked a new style of ministry to deal with it.

Amos is addressed to the rich, not as if wealth were itself wrong, but because much of the wealth in Israel had arisen through exploitation and suppression of the poor. The early part of the reign of Jeroboam II (c. 786–746 BC) had been a time of peace and prosperity in which it had been possible to re-establish the northern and southern boundary of even that part of the northern kingdom of Israel which lay to the east of the Jordan. Internally it had been a good time also, but regrettably the powerful had taken advantage of that to establish a luxurious lifestyle for themselves. Very striking excavations at Tirzah, the capital of the kingdom before Samaria and about fifteen kilometres to the east, have indicated that dwellings in the tenth-century BC – 200 years before – had been, as the law of jubilee might imply, of moderately uniform size. By Amos' day (around 762 BC) there was a section of very large and comfortable houses complemented by a crushed and squalid sector for the underdogs. As always, the blast of God's voice against such injustice does not stand in isolation, but is linked to

the criticism of individual immorality and departure from
the true worship of God which – and not only in Israel –
accompany it. The official priest responds to Amos' criticism of the worship at Bethel by indignantly speaking of it as
'the king's sanctuary and the temple of the kingdom'.[35] But
that is just the problem – God's holy place has degenerated
into the shrine of national pride and the totem of national
security.

Amos himself is a good instance of the one who has been
anointed by the Spirit of the Lord to proclaim good news to
the poor and announce liberation to the captives. Himself
not a religious professional but a middle-class farmer or
agricultural supervisor[36] from Tekoa, ten miles south of
Jerusalem, he has left his job at God's calling and travelled –
with God's usual scant regard for human national boundaries – from Judah to itinerate in Israel, protesting social
abuse and announcing judgement from God and the end of
his forbearance: 'The time is ripe for my people Israel; I will
spare them no longer.'[37]

Using freely (as only the much bigger books of the Psalms,
the Proverbs, and Isaiah also do) the full range of 'poor'
vocabulary,[38] Amos aims a number of charges at the nation's
corruption. In fact, he begins by swinging his criticisms
against an array of surrounding nations, in a way which
initially fed the self-righteousness of his hearers: *Damascus*
has come upon Gilead with crushing violence and sadistic
cruelty;[39] *Gaza* has broken up settled social units and sent the
people into slavery;[40] *Tyre* has done likewise, but worse, has
done so in violation of solemnly given agreement;[41] *Edom* has
stepped into the grip of bloodlust, not stopping even at
fratricide (and has, by the way, bought the slaves on sale
from Gaza and Tyre);[42] *Ammon*'s rampant expansionism
has been expressed in sadistic inhumanity;[43] *Moab*'s war
methods included not only regicide but dishonour to the
remains of the king and so, by implication, to the divine
institution of kingship;[44] *Judah*, Israel's southern neighbour

and partner in the *people* of Israel, has ripped up God's law and engaged in idolatry.[45]

Sweet listening, this, for the elders of the northern kingdom! But then the barrel of the cannon swings upon them . . .

> This is what the Lord says:
> For three sins of *Israel*, even for four, I will not turn back my wrath.
> They sell the righteous for silver, and the *needy* for a pair of sandals.
> They trample on the heads of the *poor* as upon the dust of the ground and deny justice to the *oppressed*. Father and son use the same girl and so profane my holy name.
> They lie down beside every altar on garments taken in pledge.
> In the house of their god they drink wine taken as fines.[46]

A number of important criticisms are here being made at once:

1. The *oppressor's attitude* is contrasted with his victim's. 'The righteous' and 'the needy' in verse 6 are in parallel, suggesting in Hebrew idiom that the two are closely congruent if not identical. This is a persistent theme which is increasingly evident in the Psalms and Proverbs. It is *not* that all poor people are automatically in the right with God, but that those who have little – especially in the context of elect Israel – are *likely* to be those who *tend* to trust the Lord. They are, socially speaking, the 'innocent party', and they are the special object of God's love; spiritually speaking, they are those who look to the Lord – where else? – for justice and help. It is not, therefore, only the vulnerable who are exploited but the godly.

2. The *motive of the oppressor* is greed – silver and even shoes are of much more worth to him than the dignity or welfare

of the suffering. He denies the command to be tender-hearted.[47] (It may be that shoes were used as symbols in land transactions – so the point is not 'even for shoes they do it' but for money and land.)

3. The *style of the oppressor* is vicious and contemptuous, treading on the needy and their feelings – as if dust.

4. The *method of the oppressor* is to seize and abuse the institutions of society whose whole *raison d'être* is to protect the people. He denies justice to the oppressed, probably passing unjust legislation[48] and then bending the judiciary to his will in explicit denial of the Torah.

5. The *personal mores of the oppressor* sink with his social ethics, again scorning the Torah and denying the dignity of women.

6. The *religion of the oppressor* loses sight of reverence and the fear of God, sleeping and drinking wine in the holy places – which are plural, possibly implying the 'high places' of Baal more than the sanctuaries of Yahweh.

7. The *heart of the oppressor is hard*, denying Deuteronomy 24:12 and retaining the poor man's cloak while he is left to shiver.

8. The *corruption of the oppressor* blurs the line between public office and private gain, so that wine taken in fines – and doubtless other public funds – is consumed in person by the holders of power. In such a situation, as commonly today, the fines have a way of growing illegally and being extorted violently, as well as of vanishing improperly into corrupt coffers.

The rest of the book enlarges and underscores the picture. This national unfaithfulness is in face of all God's faithfulness and goodness to the people, including his warnings.[49] (This is also very much the message of Hosea.) They have even tried to silence God's spokesmen and thus protect their conscience from disturbance.[50] The only effect will be the

now unavoidable judgement of God.[51] Amos himself has
been sent to speak out for God, but even him they try to
silence.[52] The affluent ladies of Samaria might be the cocktail
circle of any modern city – 'cows of Bashan . . . who oppress
the poor and crush the needy and say to your husbands,
"Bring us some drinks!" '[53] Their worship has become an
abomination because, loud and proud as it may be, it is quite
in conflict with their lives.[54] Even now Torah still calls them
to repentance, but with little hope.[55] The complaint of
corruption in the courts of law persists.[56] There is a strong
implication that injustice is, as ever, maintained by force.[57]
The plight of the poor is in contrast to the excessive luxury
and affluence for the rich with their summer and winter
houses, ivory decoration, feastings, wine and other comforts.[58] Those who long for 'the day of the Lord' – his day of
judgement and victory – are misguided, for it will not be
nationalistic victory for them, but righteous judgement
against them.[59] Their avarice breeds frustration even with
the feasts of the Lord for they are itching to get back to
commerce and exploitation.[60] God's ways and words have
been so despised that not only his blessing but his communication – now scorned but one day to be sought after – will
be withdrawn.[61] The pride of Samaria, for all its grand
mansions and civil glory, is a 'sinful kingdom':[62] so often is
the glitter of earth not of God. Nonetheless Amos, like
Jeremiah, sees beyond the judgement to the restoration in
which God's people will be sifted and the sifted saved, and
again his righteousness prevail in the land.[63]

All this is an ominous and awesome picture. The poor here
are as near identified with the materially deprived and
politically exploited as anywhere in scripture even though
that perspective is tempered by the insistence that they be
also God's righteous ones. The only way for the oppressor is
to wake up and turn; or failing turning, to be judged. As
Amos began by reviewing the surrounding nations and then
shockingly turning on Israel, so Yahweh implies that he is

equally Lord of all and addresses his social standards to
every nation: 'let justice roll on like a river, righteousness like
a never-failing stream!'[64]

Assyria was God's instrument in the promised judgement
of the northern kingdom of Israel, culminating in the sack of
Samaria in 722 BC. It was also the threat to which Isaiah of
Jerusalem referred as he also began to preach in the south
around 740 BC. The popular image of Isaiah as the prophet
of promise arises partly from a very selective, somewhat
Christmassy, reading ('a virgin shall bring forth . . . prince of
peace') and partly to the heavy stress on later chapters which
should not obscure the blunt challenge of the early parts.
Isaiah's emphasis is more on the neglect or rejection of
relationship with God, his law and his worship, yet he has
plenty to say about the poor and their treatment too. As Amos
addressed Samaria in Israel, Isaiah addresses Jerusalem
in Judah. His opening chapters are a divine indictment in
remarkably similar terms: the people have deserted the
Lord, and the twin results have been personal sin and social
corruption.[65]

The main difference is that where Amos is announcing
imminent and irreversible judgement, Isaiah calls for the
nation to repent.[66] Much of the early part of the book is set up
in the form of a law court scene with Yahweh indicting the
leaders or the people to their face:

> The Lord enters into judgement against the elders and
> leaders of his people: 'It is you who have ruined my
> vineyard; the plunder from the poor is in your houses.
> What do you mean by crushing my people and grinding
> the faces of the poor?' declares the Lord.[67]

As in Samaria, the crushing of the poor is not of economic
necessity, but to feed the luxury of the rich. The 'cows of
Bashan' have relatives in Jerusalem![68] The corrupt have
taken hold of the levers of society to pull them to their own

advantage: 'Woe to those who make unjust laws, to those who issue oppressive decrees, to deprive the poor of their rights and rob my oppressed people of justice, making widows their prey and robbing the fatherless.'[69]

In chapter 10 Isaiah provides a helpful sidelight on the meaning of 'the poor', for in a picture of the march of the Assyrians through the land and the fear and damage this causes, the prophet exclaims of one village 'Poor Anathoth!'[70] This is not a financial adjective but a sympathetic exclamation towards a community in alarm, suffering destruction, looting and rape. Affliction is a whole-life experience.

Isaiah's kingly saviour, the shoot from the stump of Jesse, has the Spirit of wisdom and understanding precisely to judge the needy with righteousness and with justice to give decisions for the poor of the earth.[71]

This theme of God's defence of his own poor and needy ones can be applied equally when they, as his nation, come under external threat. Isaiah warns the Philistines, for example, not to rejoice in the death of King Ahaz (715 BC) for this will not give them an opening to attack Judah; Yahweh himself will defend it: 'The poorest of the poor will find pasture, and the needy will lie down in safety . . . The Lord has established Zion, and in her his afflicted people will find refuge.'[72] Again, we must be wary of a flatly nationalistic interpretation, for the symbolic significance of Zion implies more – they are safe not only in a city but in reliance on the Lord who dwells there. Again one can run away from neither the practical dimension of salvation (for it was physical pasture and safety that were given) nor from the religious, for it was in Yahweh that these geographical gifts – and doubtless their spiritual counterparts – were to be found.

Precisely this counterpoise of religious trust and practical provision emerges in the lovely psalm of praise which is Isaiah 25:

O Lord, you are my God; I will exalt you and praise your
name, for in perfect faithfulness you have done marvellous
things, things planned long ago . . .
You have been a refuge for the poor, a refuge for the needy
in his distress, a shelter from the storm and a shade from
the heat. For the breath of the ruthless is like a storm
driving against a wall and like the heat of the desert.[73]

It is a song of vindication for God's people, in the midst of all
people – very New Testament!

When Zion becomes a city of pride and oppression,
God's judgement is implemented by the poor themselves as
agents of his revolution, yet again these are not just an
economic category, but one immediately re-identified as 'the
righteous', who make their way in God's home over the ruins
of pride.[74]

Judgement on the arrogant, with their constant symptoms
of empty religion, personal triviality and perversion of right,
continues to go hand in hand with the restoration of the
humble, a restoration which encompasses rejoicing in both
God himself and the fruits of his justice in society:[75] 'Once
more the humble will rejoice in the Lord . . . The ruthless will
vanish . . . those who . . . with false testimony deprive the
innocent of justice.'[76]

Whatever our view of the authorship of Isaiah (see
Appendix II) the unity of its theology is nowhere clearer than
in the concept of the poor as both the needy and those with
open hearts towards God, and in the consistent determination of Yahweh to bless, protect and restore them. In Isaiah
41:17 we find that 'The poor and needy search for water . . .
But I the Lord will answer them . . .'

In the context of scripture's use of water imagery, this
must refer to an overall longing of the heart for fulfilment –
in God, in peace, in national dignity, in relationships, in
prosperity, in justice – as much as in a drink or an irrigation
system.[77] So the vision of restored Jerusalem in these

chapters is always holistic, to do with right relationship to Yahweh, peace among the people, and physical restoration all at once. To reduce that is an insult to the high and all-embracing poetic language of this area of scripture – let alone to its context. So in Isaiah 49, following a lofty announcement of the role of God's coming servant, comes the call: 'Shout for joy, O heavens; rejoice, O earth; burst into song, O mountains! For the Lord comforts his people and will have compassion on his afflicted ones.'[78] That has to be read through the New Testament's vision of the consolation of Israel and the compassion of Jesus.

To add a shade to our comprehension of terms, it is in these sections that the term 'afflicted' means 'under the judgement of God': Jerusalem is 'poor' because God has made it so, deliberately giving it a cup to make the community stagger with his anger. Part of the restoration of the people consists in the cup being given instead to the erstwhile oppressor.[79] In this way the affliction of the judged comes to be both God's judgement and its effects (suffering and exile), just as blessing means both God's presence and the practical elimination of poverty and injustice.[80]

The link between false religion and social wrong is likewise mirrored in the link between true obedience and practical obligation in Isaiah 58's definition of fasting, much quoted (rightly) in today's oppressive situations.[81]

Yahweh's ready response to intercession hangs upon such repentance and restitution as a precondition – '*Then* you will call, and the Lord will answer . . .'[82]

We come to Isaiah 61. The first phrases we have already referred to in connection with Luke 4 (p. 25ff.); it is enough here to add that the context underlines the truth visible throughout Isaiah, that we are dealing here with a holistic answer to poverty, running from the knowledge of the Lord right across to lands, fields and lawcourts. Certainly it is a national vision, even nationalistic in conceiving of neighbouring aliens coming to do the Jews' manual labour for them; yet it is still a vision of a nation *under God*, set free not only for material prosperity or right social relations, but for the worship, service and love of God. Perhaps nowhere, except in Jesus, is the fusion of these various dimensions of salvation more eloquent:

> They will rebuild the ancient ruins . . .
> Aliens will shepherd your flocks . . .
> You will be called priests of the Lord, you will be named ministers of our God . . . my people will inherit a double portion in their land, and everlasting joy will be theirs.
> For I, the Lord, love justice;
> I hate robbery and iniquity.
> In my faithfulness I will . . . make an everlasting covenant with them . . .
> I delight greatly in the Lord; my soul rejoices in my God.[83]

Practical, yes – but as ever, in Zion. Lest we miss the point – or lest they in national fervour do so – the final chapter returns to it concisely: 'This is the one I esteem: he who is humble and contrite in spirit, and *trembles at my word*.'[84] The effect of that will be righteous moral and social behaviour: but the root of it is religious, an attitude of heart before the Lord. Such are God's poor.

While many of the other prophets are dealing in various ways with this theme, they do so less directly than Amos and Isaiah. None presents the correlation of God's love for the oppressed and the poor's need to love God so clearly or eloquently as Isaiah. Their testimony is nevertheless unanimous around the same cluster of truths. Zephaniah is probably nearest to Isaiah's spirit, as he is also earliest in time, writing before the reforms of Josiah (in 621 BC) which Jeremiah saw. He joins the chorus of criticism of those who operate unjustly – 'Woe to the city of oppressors' – yet he is noticeably aware of Isaiah's conviction, that the poor whom God loves are not only the needy, but those whose need has led them to an open attitude towards him. The right response to the coming day of the Lord (a day of both joy and judgement) is to seek the Lord and *do what he commands*. When God promises restoration to those 'who trust in the name of the Lord', freedom from insecurity is part of the deal, for God's love is not for the materially poor in isolation, but for the humble, dependent, trusting poor, open to God if his hand is to be fully open to them.[85]

Jeremiah, writing in Jerusalem at the time when God's threat of Babylonian invasion is about to become reality, opens with some very similar indictments to Isaiah's. His emphasis is perhaps more leaning on the root of the problem, the people's idolatry and neglect of God: yet he also pinpoints the end fruit 'You of this generation . . . On your clothes men find the lifeblood of the innocent poor'.[86] There is the same anger with those whose wealth is made on the backs of the poor and enforced through a bent judiciary.[87] There is the same awareness of Yahweh as intrinsically the champion of the underdog.[88]

There is, too, the Old Testament's common stress on the fact that kings are to be rulers after God's heart and to implement his longing to restrain the wicked and protect the poor. Jeremiah addresses Jehoahaz (Shallum) in chapter 22 and contrasts him with his outstanding reformist father, Josiah:

> He did what was right and just, so all went well with him.
> He defended the cause of the poor and needy, and so all went well.
> Is that not what it means to know me? . . .
> But your eyes and your heart are set only on dishonest gain, on shedding innocent blood and on oppression and extortion.[89]

While Jeremiah was left in Jerusalem, his younger contemporary Ezekiel was freighted off to Babylon, where he

prophesied among the exiled community. In his extended
allegorical judgement on Jerusalem he accuses her of being
worse than her older sister, Samaria[90] (Amos has shown us
what that means), and her younger sister Sodom whose
people were arrogant, over-fed and unconcerned; they did
not help the poor and needy. Again, in his famous treatment
of personal responsibilities before God (the 'sour grapes'
passage of Ezekiel 18) his description of the man who will not
live, whose 'blood will be upon his own head', is:

> He eats at the mountain shrines.
> He defiles his neighbour's wife.
> He oppresses the poor and needy.
> He commits robbery.
> He does not return what he took in pledge.
> He looks to the idols.
> He does detestable things.
> He lends at usury and takes excessive interest.[91]

By contrast his righteous son avoids both idolatry and
personal immorality, and also 'does not oppress anyone . . .
but gives his food to the hungry and provides clothing for the
naked'.[92]

As so often it is the nation's leadership which is at fault.
Ezekiel's critique of them is well known from the 'careless
shepherds' passage of chapter 34, but is just as explicit in his
vision of Judah as a dry and barren land, 'a land that has had
no rain or showers in the day of wrath'.[93] In this land,

> There is a conspiracy of her princes . . . they devour people
> . . . Her priests do violence to my law . . . her officials . . . are
> like wolves tearing their prey; they shed blood and kill
> people to make unjust gain. Her prophets whitewash these
> deeds . . . The people of the land (having been set such a
> fine example!) practise extortion and commit robbery;
> they oppress the poor and needy and mistreat the alien,
> denying them justice.[94]

In these last verses Ezekiel homes right in to Deuteronomy –
and maybe gives us a clue as to why Jesus Christ owed
so much to the book. The above translation is from the
Septuagint; maybe the Hebrew is nearer the truth with its
allusive 'the land has not been *cleansed* or rained on'. Many a
land is in that place.

It is just this concern with earlier Torah, given and disregarded, which fires the indignation of Zechariah, writing
after the exile when the restoration of Jerusalem was under
way: 'This is what the Lord Almighty says: "Administer true
justice; show mercy and compassion to one another. Do not
oppress the widow or the fatherless, the alien or the poor." '[95]
He too, however, has held onto Isaiah's double reference of
poverty to both need and simplicity of heart. Even the
coming king will not only care for the downtrodden; he will
partake of their simple and trustful attitude of spirit towards
Yahweh, 'your king comes to you, righteous and having
salvation, gentle (*anaw*) and riding on a donkey'.[96]

Zechariah also works with the imagery of Yahweh as
shepherd of the flock, not only blessing as in Ezekiel 34, but
judging and rejecting when the flock rebelled: 'I pastured the
flock marked for slaughter, particularly the oppressed of the
flock . . . Then I took my staff marked Favour and broke it,
revoking the covenant I had made . . . the afflicted of the flock
who were watching me knew it was the word of the Lord.'[97]
When the king did come, righteous and having salvation, it
was both to set free the oppressed and to seek God's righteous
poor, 'the meek and humble, who trust in the name of the
Lord'.[98]

The poor in the writings

The third section of the Hebrew Bible, after the law and
the prophets, was known as the writings. At first sight this
is a motley collection, but several factors hold it together as

a species of literature. For one, it is more self-consciously literary than much of the Old Testament: it contains large tracts of poetry (the Psalms), collections of sayings taken over from other cultures and re-theologised (much of Proverbs), sustained reflective debates about key issues in life (Job, Ecclesiastes), and so forth. The stance adopted by the writers on the question of the poor is substantially identical to the rest of the Old Testament.

No hymn is great without great theology. The greatest hymn collection ever made, the book of the Psalms, is the supreme example. Along with its sublime vision of God, its sharp perception of man in his folly, its soaring language and its crunching relevance, it passes frequent and perceptive comment on the matter of the poor. 'Frequent' means that the various terms arise sixty-six times, thirty-seven being the root *ani*.[99]

The main principles which emerge are:

1. *God is for the oppressed, afflicted and needy*. God's basic response of love to the plight of the poor and disadvantaged is the point of departure: 'he does not ignore the cry of the *afflicted*'.[100]

It is constantly reiterated that the wicked are marked by their oppressive behaviour to the poor and defenceless, and that Yahweh is set to reverse their fortunes, casting down the mighty from their seat and exalting the humble and weak.[101]

2. *The poor, however, tends to mean the godly poor*. Here as elsewhere there is an ambiguity in the use of the language, so that those who are materially poor are often also credited with faith, and so that one is often unsure whether material state or attitude of heart is in view. The parallelism – very much a device in Hebrew writing – is especially close in Psalm 37:14, 'The wicked draw the sword and bend the bow to bring down the *poor and needy*, to slay those whose *ways are upright*.'[102]

In Psalm 69 the refrain comes again – that those who are afflicted are likely to be seekers after God, those whose hearts lift at the sound of the strains of worship: 'I will praise God's name in song . . . The poor will see and be glad – you who seek God, may your hearts live! The Lord hears the needy . . .'[103] Here the God who 'proclaims release to the captives' does so first for their incarcerated hearts, though then – quite clearly – for their imprisoned community. This is just because it is those whose hearts are right that he delights to bless in more visible ways: 'You save the humble but bring low those whose eyes are haughty.'[104]

The poor, in a word, are those who take the Lord as *their* God, whom he delights to call *his people*; and they are, embarrassingly, often to be found among the humbler ranks of the community. 'For the Lord takes delight in *his people*; he crowns the *humble* with salvation.'[105]

3. *Men are expected to act justly.* One corollary of God's love for the poor is that those who hate or exploit them are out of order. The actions of the wicked are repeatedly contrasted with what God will do by way of retribution and restitution. The king, on the other hand, is meant to be an extension of God's attitude, and is, therefore, to defend and promote the poor and their rights – no wonder that function fell afresh to the Son of David.[106]

4. *'Poor' can be a spiritual state.* Again and again the psalmist describes himself as 'afflicted' or 'cast down' and one can only believe it has to do with his lack of inner wellbeing. It is obviously related to rough circumstances on some occasions, and it is clearly tied to the heavy hand of God's judgement on others. It is too feeble to think only of mood; this is a state not only brought to God, but brought about by his presence and awesome reality. It is a cry which has to issue in a plea for God's grace to relieve it through a knowledge of his loving presence: no lesser spiritual reality can solve it. Outward

stress may breed such inner distress, but it is a cry from the
spirit of a man who knows God: the man who has never
known that thirst, or something like it, has yet to qualify as
one of the Lord's poor. Without that, liberationist he may be,
but liberated he is not in sight of becoming.[107]

5. *'Poor' can also be an emotional state*. This is not so far from the
point above, for all our make-up is one, and distress spills
from one part of us to another; but the point is worth making
separately, for it reminds us not only of the range of human
distress which may be brought to God, but also of the
breadth of *his* compassion which meets it, as in Jesus. Maybe
the clearest single instance is in the title to Psalm 102, 'A
prayer of an afflicted man. When he is faint and pours out his
lament before the Lord.' We shall be reminded in the gospels
of the response of Christ's compassion to just such varied
human pains. It is simply explained – he is the Son of a
Father just like that.

The Proverbs are a most remarkable gathering up of wit
and wisdom, much of it from *The Wisdom of Amenemope* from
Egypt but translated into the language of Israel to show that
all true wisdom flows from Yahweh. There is considerable
treatment of the poor, and it makes much the same points as
the Psalms. There is again the ambiguity which highlights
his love, both for those at the bottom of the pile and for those
who are reverently responsive to himself. It is again emphasised that a lowly spirit is appropriate before God, even if it
denies one the fruits of self-confidence.[108]

Again there are clear social responsibilities to the poor,
simply put: 'The righteous care about justice for the poor!'[109]
The famous good wife of Proverbs 31 'opens her arms to the
poor and extends her hands to the needy'.[110]

The ruler too has a special responsibility, for 'A ruler
who oppresses the poor is like a driving rain that leaves no
crops . . . Like a roaring lion or a charging bear is a wicked

man ruling over a helpless people . . . If a king judges the poor with fairness, his throne will always be secure.'[111]

Two fresh points do emerge in the Proverbs, the first of which is a dramatic hint of Yahweh's deep identification with the poor: 'He who oppresses the poor shows contempt for their Maker, but whoever is kind to the needy honours God.'[112] It is hard to believe that this was not in the mind of the storyteller of Matthew 25:31–46. The other, in the mouth of a righteous man, is a subtle point made in prayer:

> Two things I ask of you, O Lord; do not refuse me before I die:
> Keep falsehood and lies far from me; give me neither poverty nor riches, but give me only my daily bread.
> Otherwise, I may have too much and disown you and say, 'Who is the Lord?'
> Or I may become poor and steal, and so dishonour the name of my God.[113]

Materialism is rejected for it may stand between a man and his God; so much we know well, and read in our New Testament. But poverty is dangerous for it too may lead a man away from God. This is an important point, for those who abominate materialism and wealth can readily romanticise poverty. The Bible has more common sense than that. Precisely one of the theological points in this book is that there is no salvation by poverty, whether compulsory or via the 'simple lifestyle'. While God loves the poor, and in a special way, that is by no means to sanctify poverty or oppression as if God were to choose one special group for automatic salvation. It is neither so simple, nor so trite.

It is not possible to pass by the book of Job, though it is important to watch the context lest the statements one reads are in the mouth of one of the advisers who had his thinking wrong and is deliberately presented to us as a caricature. In one way Job is especially about the poor, for the whole book is in a way an extended debate about the Protestant ethic (that is, the idea that if you are godly God will bless you materially – and you had better work hard to be sure of it!). The 'plot' of course, concerns the removal of Job's goods, then his health, to test his attitude to God, and the book consists of a debate about why it has all really happened. It is remarkable, in this context, to see the same basic theology shining through.

In one of his fits of frustration, for example, Job wonders why God is so slow to enact justice – but he does so on the presumption that God is just, loves justice, and longs to bring it about.[114] Elihu shares his conviction though maybe oversimplifies the very thing that is bothering Job.[115] The obligation of good men to act for the poor is clearly stated, if only in Job's rather self-righteous apologia, 'I rescued the poor who cried for help.'[116] As with Proverbs there is the deeper perception that 'hardship does you good' is all too trivial a doctrine – for that very reason it is placed on the lips of Elihu, verbatim.[117] Job's comforters have been justly called 'an extended illustration of the Anglican approach to counselling'!

Finally, just one realistic remark from the sceptical pen of Ecclesiastes: 'If you see the poor oppressed in a district, and justice and rights denied, do not be surprised at such things; for one official is eyed by a higher one, and over them both are others higher still.'[118] As he says, there is nothing new under the sun.

To sum up, although there are spiritual rebels among the poor and humble souls among the wealthy, the Old Testament maintains that there is a persistent link between material wellbeing and spiritual self-sufficiency. For this reason the Bible regards the poor as *tending* to be humble and open towards God, and the rich as *tending* to ignore him: the distance between the poor and the poor in spirit is not as great as we thought, though the distinction is real. And while we do need to study the differences between one kind of poor and another to disentangle our present-day theology, they do have a tendency to move together in concept; which greatly simplifies our problem.

The Spirit of the Lord

When Jesus set about announcing good news for these poor, he knew that he needed the Spirit of the Lord to enable him to do it. There is a certain anonymity, even vagueness, about the Holy Spirit in the Old Testament largely because he is specifically 'the Spirit of Jesus'.[119] It therefore needs the New Testament's announcement of Jesus to give much content to the concept of the Spirit. Further, it needs the ministry of Jesus before – logically and chronologically before – that of the Spirit can be fully unlocked. This is so much so that John can say, 'Up to that time the Spirit had not been given (some translations: 'There *was no Holy Spirit*'), since Jesus had not yet been glorified.'[120]

Nevertheless we need to know what Jesus' mind owed to the Old Testament's understanding of the Spirit. In much of the Old Testament language is used indistinctly, not to confuse but to enrich the understanding with allusive and poetic usage. So, for instance, the basic Hebrew word *ruach* serves for wind, breath, spirit, or divine power, a series of thoughts on which Jesus draws in John 3:8. Thus the rushing power of wind over the land and the human life which God breathes into our bodies and the spiritual power which he displays in prophet, priest or king are all closely related.[121] The rich effect of that appears in a towering poetic passage like Genesis 1:2, where God's breath – the storm? the Spirit? the lifegiving air? – hovers over the deeps of the formless, empty creation. The root idea is that of rushing power flowing from the being of God, and manifesting itself in different mighty ways in the world and the lives of men. Because this Spirit flows over and into men, the ambivalence

of wind-breath-Spirit is complemented by a further ambivalence in which it is often far from clear, when God's Spirit
moves upon man's, whether the Old Testament is referring
by *ruach* to God's power or the spiritual equipment of man by
which he relates to God.

This dynamic power, breathed by God, has several Old
Testament fruits. It is this which gives man life – in every
sense from physical to supernatural: he is only human
because the life God has given to him is Life, unique and
divinely related, setting him off from the rest of creation.[122]
It is this which moves the creation as such, disturbing the
elements affecting the seasons and conditions on the land,
and forwarding God's plans in history.[123] It is this which
grants creativity and skill to men.[124]

This same dynamic falls upon Israel's leaders, for many
ends but specifically to enable spiritual insight and spokes-
manship for God[125] and for wise and powerful leadership.[126]
As the people became increasingly settled, it seems that the
act of anointing leaders (kings and priests especially) with oil
was coterminous with God's gift of the Spirit for leadership.
This is not to say that anointing effected the coming of the
Spirit, nor that the Spirit was confined to the anointed; but
it was assumed that those emerging as leaders were God's
chosen, that his Spirit was thus their prerogative as well as
their necessary resource, and that anointing was both
appropriate as expressing this authority and also somehow
confirmatory, if not instrumental, in the Spirit's coming.[127]

Sadly the assumption that God's power would be available to leaders from generation to generation fostered
spiritual complacency. As a result many of the conflicts in
the Old Testament arise because God has sent an unlikely
spokesman, under his Spirit, to challenge the effete conduct
of social or religious life, and the establishment cannot
conceive of their own anointed approach being defective nor
of anyone else having God's right to challenge them.[128] This
may explain the rather curious reluctance of the eighth- and

ninth-century prophets to claim God's Spirit explicitly as
their authority, preferring rather to speak of God's hand or
word; maybe the claim to be under God's Spirit was a little
too faded and well-worn in the corridors of tradition.[129]
What mattered was authenticity, not the grounds on which
they defended it. This sense that the Spirit was handed down
through the cult, the temple, the teachers and the priests,
and that thus the will of the Spirit would be identified with
the voice of the religious establishment, was taken a step
further after the close of the Old Testament. By Jesus' day,
the rabbis of Judaism were not only confusing what they
taught *ipso facto* with the voice of the Spirit; they were saying
that the Torah, the law teaching for Israel, so embodied the
word of the Spirit that he virtually had no role besides it. He
was, indeed, the Spirit of prophecy, but of the great prophets
long ago, not of a living voice for their day. His voice was
thus all the more 'bottled up' in the traditions they sought
to expound. (There is a contemporary parallel here too.) It
was only weird charismatics like the Qumran community
who spoke as if the Spirit were a vivid or vocal reality to
them, and they were apocalyptic fanatics. All the more is
Jesus therefore identified with the Spirit of Isaiah and the
other prophets in Luke 4, not only in the obvious claim to be
so but in the implication that he, like them, was willing and
authorised under God's Spirit to challenge the status quo
and its servants.

The dynamic of God's Spirit, and especially his role in
speaking the word of promise and consolation, seems to have
been rediscovered during and after the exile in Babylon (for
most of the community this was 597–539 BC). This makes
spiritual sense. The complacency of the people, their ensuing
trust in buildings and traditions, their arrant assumption of
God's defence by a kind of totemic possession of God by
Israel, were smashed. Searching questions were asked and
issues of religious loyalty faced. Thus the prophetic assur-
ance that God's promise and his Torah would not fail is

coupled with the Spirit's ministry.[130] The young Ezekiel, in Babylon while his older contemporary Jeremiah was still active in Jerusalem, was sharply aware of the Spirit as his inspiration along with God's message itself.[131] The writings, which seem to have been put together at this time, speak of God's wisdom in an almost personified way as the means by which he communicates promise and truth – yet this too is the fruit of the Spirit's dynamic; wisdom may be the analogy, the Spirit is the fact. In Proverbs 1:23, for example, in the opening appeal for men to listen, 'Wisdom' is saying, 'If you had responded to my rebuke, I would have poured out my heart (or *Spirit*) to you and made my thoughts known to you.'

Since the Spirit's ministry is often to teach, to challenge and to correct, even when it means confronting all the 'official prophets' of the day, it will not surprise us that he is seen with an ethical character. The title 'Holy' is rare, and the emphasis is on power more than purity; nonetheless the implied demand that on meeting the Spirit man must take account of God's holiness is everywhere to be found. This is congruent with the message of every prophet. It comes explicitly in the confession of David;[132] an abiding challenge to the worshipping community whatever the literary history of the psalm. The reminiscence of Isaiah, 'they rebelled and grieved his Holy Spirit', is in the context of one of those sustained historical analyses in which the prophets often set the charges of the Lord against his people.[133] This was their way, and God's was an unavoidable reaction: rebellion against him by definition is grief to the Spirit. Similarly, a spirit of submission to God is rightly aligned with the belief that in such the Spirit of the Lord will gladly teach and guide: 'Teach me to do your will, for you are my God; may your good Spirit lead me on level ground.'[134]

God's Spirit was also the breath of hope. Much of the Old Testament's reference to the Spirit is forward-looking. This is true both of the hoped-for messianic figure upon whom the Spirit was expected to rest in singular power,[135] and of the work of the Spirit for God's people themselves. The long awaited, unavoidably needed new relationship with God which he had promised to inaugurate, in which the law and power of God would be internalised, included the promise: 'I will . . . put a new spirit in you.'[136] In this renovating revolution of the last days God would release his power from above with productive and potent effect.[137] The agent of this new event, whether seen as prophet, Messiah or Israel as a whole, would act under this same Spirit.[138]

Taking this altogether, we can see the depth of Isaiah 61:1–2 and the reason Jesus chose to quote it. For when Isaiah speaks of the Spirit upon him, whether he has in mind his own prophetic experience, or the calling of Israel as a whole, or the single divine servant of the longed-for future (and any or all of these could be right understandings of his mind), he had certain clear notions of what that entailed. It implied that the fire and rushing power of God was upon him; that he was no longer but a man among men, debating or persuading or working as other men, but additionally an agent of the Most High, enabled to act and speak with peculiar authority and effect. His touch could cut through dead wood, speak directly to the heart, cause life to flower and hope to grow and situations to change: for that was ever the effect of God's breath. It implied that he stood where the chosen leaders stood, with insight into man and awareness of the heartbeat and longings of God. It implied a vision of the future and a freedom to announce it. It implied a kinship with David and Samuel and Moses, with Amos and Micaiah ben Imlah and Nathan: spokesmen of the Lord, set apart and authorised to lead. It implied an authority extraneous to the institutions of Israel, though entirely akin to their roots, out of which deviation from the Lord on the part of others could be confronted. It implied being a mouthpiece: one who could secure by his words an exodus from Egypt, repentance from a king, the defeat of an army or the restoration of a city. It implied the right to announce God's word, whether of promise, of warning, or of truth, to all who needed it, from kings to paupers and from pious to pagans. And for those who would hear it, it would be freedom and sight and release, the breathing-on of the Lord's favour, good news to all. Out of such a flame would the prophet of Nazareth blaze.

4 PRIORITIES PRACTISED

Solly Menachemson, of course, knew all that Old Testament stuff – but through the nationalistic spectacles of his people. Oddly enough, Fanie was in just the same position – so much of that book had been in the past related to the national history and aspirations of Afrikanerdom. Both of them had missed the universal implications of that teaching, together with its relevance to the poor, the needy, the underdog and the racial alien. Those were the bits which had precisely not been lost on the sharp mind and political awareness of a Zipho Selele, whose challenge to Simon's apparently middle-class faith came in terms of its danger of spiritualising all the really vital issues. It all made Simon deeply disturbed, for he had no desire to embrace a distorted faith, nor to desert the many of the poor as he knew them; yet he battled to believe that the material implications of God's gospel could be the whole story, not least because of the depth of his own experience of God, the joy of forgiveness, the wonder of prayer and the reality of worship. Somehow the two – the reality of God and the needs of the world – had to belong together.

If we are to help their debate, we need to look not only at Jesus' words in Nazareth and the biblical background to them, but at what he proceeded to do. If he really thought he was sent to proclaim God's good news to the poor in the power of the divine Spirit, what he actually did should give us the very insight into the balance of his ministry which we need to grasp and carry forward into today's church. In this chapter we follow Luke's account of Jesus' work, with sideways glances to the other gospels, to see *whom Jesus actually dealt with* and *how*, to see whom he regarded as the poor and what he conceived God's message for them to be.

Preliminaries to the public ministry

By way of overture, there are three little dramas by which Luke sets the scene before Jesus' public ministry begins, and which are instructive for our purposes: the nativity accounts, the work of John, and the testing of Jesus in the desert.

The nativity story. People differ as to whether the nativity accounts were originally Luke's work or whether he found the tales already created and simply incorporated them into his work as a fitting and attractive introduction. For the latter case is argued the different style and language of the first two chapters of his gospel; for the former, the fact that the content is so different anyway, that it would unavoidably give rise to different vocabulary and manner of telling. The same people will differ over the status of these passages, whether they are – or indeed were ever meant to be – of the same objective historical character as Luke claims for his work as a whole, or whether they are (to use that slippery term) myths received from imaginative and poetic quarters, inserted more from theological considerations than gynaecological veracity. For our purposes we need primarily to grasp what Luke was wanting us to hear at this point.

The first and most obvious point, which resists any of today's attempts to impose a twentieth-century agenda on the gospel material, is that Luke is concerned with *the initiative of God in fulfilling his plan for mankind*. That, and the two figures to whom it gives rise – John and Jesus – are centre stage, not the nature or identity (and still less the merits) of any of the other actors. Zechariah has his once-in-a-lifetime opportunity as priest to offer the incense in the temple; at this high point in his life God (typically) meets him with a promise – but wholly and dumbfoundingly unexpectedly. Zechariah had nothing to do with it: 'I,' says the angel, 'have been sent to speak to you.'[1] Just as unbidden, God's messenger appears in Mary's kitchen and in the Bethlehem fields to the shepherds. Even to Simeon and Anna[2] the news of God breaks as long-awaited, longed-for and promised but at that moment unexpected. As ever in the scriptures God breaks in at his own behest, sending his man to 'go on before the Lord . . . to make ready a people prepared', ready for the 'good news of great joy that will be for all the people . . . a Saviour . . . Christ the Lord'.[3] God is the agent, Jesus the focus, John the forerunner; the rest is scenery.

It is not, though, scenery without significance. Luke pointedly lets us know what Isaiah has led us to expect, namely that the people God chooses to deal with are the needy, the lowly and the brokenhearted. Zechariah and Elizabeth bore the stigma of childlessness, and John was (if only incidentally, nonetheless really) 'a joy and delight *to you*' and an answer to their prayers.[4] Mary and Joseph are so poor that when they come to offer the sacrifice prescribed at the time of purification after childbirth, they have to take advantage of the concession to bring a pair of doves or two young pigeons instead of the normal lamb.[5] It is not only overcrowding which causes the poignant scene at the inn door in Bethlehem, but their lack of financial clout. It is entirely in keeping that God then summons the ill-thought-of manual workers from the night shift to be the first to see the king in the feeding trough. And although nothing is said directly about their material circumstances, much the same applies to God's choice of an old man in sight of death and an aged widow[6] to receive the revelation in the temple of this new child's identity.

Even here, however, in these picturesque chapters, Luke does not lose sight of the Old Testament's stress on the *godly* poor as distinct from just the materially needy. Except for the shepherds, there is a broad hint that each of the other actors here is a person open to God; not meritorious necessarily, but receptive. Zechariah and Elizabeth were 'upright in the sight of God, observing all the Lord's commandments and regulations blamelessly';[7] they were people of prayer,[8] and Elizabeth is found prophesying,[9] as much as her husband.[10] When Mary is introduced her spiritual state is unmentioned (studiously?) until God's message has come to her – but then her immediate self-description as the Lord's servant, and her exemplary openness to God's future for her, 'May it be to me as you have said',[11] are meant to suggest the kind of person she was beforehand as much as after. She and Joseph jointly respond to God both in the event of her pregnancy and in the offerings and festivals which follow.[12] Simeon likewise was 'righteous and devout', and a threefold mention of God's Holy Spirit clusters round his story;[13] Anna is similar.[14]

In short, the overture prefaces the symphony: God is breaking into the life of the world in the kingly person of his Son, reaching out to the poor of every kind, looking for and working through those who are open to himself. As Mary puts it, 'my spirit rejoices in God . . . His mercy extends to those who fear him . . . He has performed mighty deeds . . . scattered those who are proud . . . brought down rulers . . . lifted up the humble . . . filled the hungry . . . sent the rich away empty'.[15] Her Magnificat bears both a more literal challenge than the incanted version beloved of middle-class Anglicanism, and more spiritual depth than perceived by the South American dictatorships which in recent years have banned its singing.

The ministry of John. As we have seen, John was sent to plough a furrow for his cousin to sow. The contrast in their personal lifestyles has often led to an exaggeration of the distinction between their ministries, as if John did the surgery and Jesus added the ointment; but that is to press the distinction too far. John's word was known as good news,[16] just as his cousin's was incisive. Certainly he preached a baptism of repentance, but it was *for the forgiveness of sins* – that was the goal, and the repentance merely the needle's eye through which it must be approached.[17] He was announcing a new relationship with the God of Israel, freedom from guilt and shame, new dignity and self-respect in the knowledge of God. Of course the repentance was to be real – his hearers were not only to pass through the waters but to produce fruit in keeping with repentance;[18] their lives had to change. And knowing the Old Testament's amalgam of sin as covering the idolatry of religious deviation, the immorality of personal wickedness and the injustice of social exploitation, they knew very well what they had to repent about and how wide a thing it was. John's *didache*, his teaching which guided his followers after they had embraced his *kerygma*, the initial proclamation, rubbed that in – the fruit included compassion for the cold and hungry, justice, sensitivity and renouncing the abuse of financial or military power.[19]

The testing of Jesus. Although Jesus knew God and his Spirit from an early age, it was out of the dramatic commissioning in his Jordan baptism that he could say 'The Spirit of the Lord is on me'.[20] It is striking, then, that before Jesus announces the fact in Nazareth, the same Spirit draws him into the chosen environment of John, the quiet harshness of the desert, to complete his preparation for the imminent explosion into ministry. It was not that he went *to meet* the devil, but that as the Spirit led him (presumably into a reflective retreat) 'he was (in the process) tempted by the devil'.[21] The precise thrust of his temptations gives Lenten preachers headaches, but their general drift is clear.

   The first – 'tell this stone to become bread' – is to do with the abuse of Christ's power and authority as the newly-commissioned Son of God to effect changes in the material world. It has something to do with the misdirection of his authority, something to do with spiritual versus material priorities (viz. the reply – 'Man does not live on bread alone'), something to do with personal greed, something to do with the route his ministry should take, whether in miraculous exhibitionism or in slower and more costly paths. What is clear is that Jesus renounces in one shot both his personal comfort, a short-cut to success and popularity, and a manifesto designed around men's material needs in isolation from the nurture of their inner being. If this account carries weight with us, Dorcas Selele's need is no more wholly met by sufficient bread than Alice Barrington's by her glut of it; they both need something more.

The second test is the supreme challenge to Jesus' own assertion that his kingdom is not of this world. Satan shows him 'in an instant all the kingdoms of the world' – to be had on impossible terms. Yet we should not over-spiritualise this issue: Jesus was not turning his back on this world, but on the running of it on Satan's terms. Even his kingdom being of another world is not a programme for pietism, for his ministry rather revolved around the announcement of the arrival of his kingdom upon this earth, in the coming of his own person. It is precisely the kingship of he who comes from beyond being effected in the here and now of earth which *is* 'the kingdom of God' in New Testament teaching. That is precisely why the offer of the devil is unacceptable, for it presupposes the use of power by the earth's criteria and in pursuit of the earth's values as formed by the miasmic influence of the devil himself: that way lie the very things John called his peers to forsake. This is why today's church has so much trouble building the kingdom. For some the need to effect its ways on the earth sucks the workers into earth's priorities and methodology; for others that very danger breeds the overreaction into subChristian pietism. As Luther had it, 'If you preach the gospel in every particular except those which affect the issues of your day, you are not preaching the gospel at all.' Corybantic Chapel and

Emmanuel Presby can lean so far out of opposite sides of the boat that they can no longer recognise each other's efforts at navigation as seaworthy sailing at all. To worship God 'and serve him only'[22] requires a very precise ear for the call to service that he is actually issuing.

The third test, on the pinnacle of the temple, is about method. Satan may have been angling for Jesus' self-destruction, but he puts it in terms of the fruits to be drawn from miraculous sensationalism – and that Jesus renounces. It would be too easy to say that Jesus renounced all striking use of power, for his protection of the 'messianic secret' has often been overdone by scholars. There is no doubt that along with it he was actually out, in the early stages at least, to create maximum impact so that the Galilee community at least would be rapidly and dramatically faced with the question of his identity. Nevertheless his response to the devil is clear: it is not enough to have a mandate to use God's power, it must be – both in general and in each situation – used only according to the Father's specific will and guidance. To presume upon it is to court disaster. So for today's church, it will not do simply to seek the miraculous release of God's power; there has to be that listening to God, that discipleship, sacrifice and obedience at cost which authenticates and controls the source and use of the power.

The recipients of the ministry

The poor untaught. Turning now to Jesus' ministry itself and starting to look at the categories of people to whom he ministered, it is unavoidable that he spent a great amount of his time in preaching and teaching. He had, after all, announced that he was anointed 'to preach . . . to *proclaim* freedom . . . recovery of sight . . . the year of the Lord's favour'.[23] Despite the anti-proclamation lobby in the church, there is no question that the ministry of Jesus was very substantially *verbal*. People had holes in their minds and perceptions which he knew he had to fill; and the core of what he proclaimed had to do with himself. There can be no kingdom ethics or kingdom teaching without the king; New Testament ethics do not exist without New Testament presuppositions. And however uncomfortable we find it, that is how Jesus spoke. These assertions need to be amplified, justified and illustrated; but I want to maintain very clearly that there was, in Jesus' mind, no greater category of the poor than those whose *understanding* needed to be enriched with the knowledge of what God was doing in their day in the person of the preacher himself. This is not the whole story, but it is the only honest place at which to begin.

That, of course, is because Luke himself begins there; his headline for Jesus' ministry is that he returned in the power of the Spirit and *taught* in their synagogues.[24] He then illustrates this with the incident at Nazareth in which those taught include his own fellow-villagers, synagogue leaders, nationalists, and traditionalists, young and old of both sexes – to name but a few of the overlapping groups present. The thrust of his message *taught* their assumptions in an assortment of different ways – just so as they saw the central significance of Jesus himself, challenging and correcting their assortment of differing viewpoints. It was, of course, not only the individuals but synagogues themselves which needed teaching – the assumptions and perspectives of the institutions of Judaism. That being so, Luke doesn't surprise us by portraying Jesus moving straight from Nazareth into the much grander synagogue at Capernaum, where his style of teaching, his deliverance of an oppressed man and the doing of it on the sabbath all challenged their traditional expectations of a synagogue meeting. The poor here were both the congregation and the delivered man, though it is striking that the deliverance was not seen as a separate ministry but as part of 'the word' – the revelatory event – of which the congregation asked, 'What is this teaching?'[25]

The habitual nature of Jesus' synagogue ministry is underlined in the closing words of the chapter[26] in which Jesus is described, having resisted the pressure of his team to stay in Capernaum, as touring 'the other towns also' and having 'kept on preaching in the synagogues of Judea'. The geographical note has many manuscript variants ('Galilee', 'the land of the Jews') – but the very difficulty of 'Judea' here should caution us against excising it, and remind us instead that Jesus' ministry probably included a number of early forays to the south of Galilee (as John's account also suggests), and that his early work was quite possibly both more widespread and more verbally explicit in the heartlands of Jewish worship than we often fancy. And he did that because there was, in his eyes, a poverty of mind in the nation that needed good news preached to it.

The synagogue, however, was far too limiting an environment for Jesus. We immediately find him standing by the lakeside with the crowds 'listening to the word of God'.[27] The poor hearers are dealt with both in bulk – by the delightful device of turning the beach into an amphitheatre and preaching from the boat – and one by one with the fishermen when 'he had finished speaking' (that is publicly).[28] The good news proved to be both fish, and the end of their fishing.[29] It might just be possible to impose a liberationist interpretation on the incident (protein for the workers . . .) if it were not for Peter's response, 'Go away from me, Lord; I am a sinful man!'[30] – Jesus himself remains the good news.

The widespread ripples, even of Jesus' earliest ministry, are clear when we find that teachers from Jerusalem are listening in as he is teaching[31] – even in the informal context of the home. They too, for all their background, are the poor – and they get more teaching than they anticipate when Jesus directs his exposition of his actions towards the paralysed man directly to them. Their unspoken, 'Who does he think he is?' is precisely the question at issue through the gospel account: Who is this, and by what right does he act? The poor, for Jesus, are those who need to know the answer to that. Revelation is in process when the response develops, 'We have seen remarkable things'.[32]

Household revelation continues over dinner at Matthew Levi's (what kind of poor *he* is, we pick up on page 112). Now the Pharisaic questions are spoken, if only in criticism – and the response teaches. He has come to *call* the poor, and if the self-styled righteous cannot see themselves among them, they will miss him; indeed they look like doing just that, for if they of all people cannot see the messianic wedding-feast when it is laid,[33] they will miss the new as well as the good. Christ's disruption of their hidebound habits is merely perceived as a threat, beyond which most of the Pharisees could never see the very wealth of his presence, the liberation that he brought in seizing back God's gift of the sabbath as a love-gift for man[34] and setting that love above the distortion of Torah in their regulations.[35] As he taught the teachable, sadly it was the teachers who were least so.

It is in keeping with the target which Jesus made of people's minds and understandings that we are given so much of his actual teaching; yet that should not fool us into imagining that merely the comprehension of his words was his goal. Our prejudice against preaching is largely that we have disjoined it from life and action. It is here that the South American theologians have done the church such a service in coining the term 'orthopraxy' to complement the West's cerebral obsession with orthodoxy. There is no reception of Jesus' teaching in isolation from obedience, which can begin to be called Christian discipleship: it is but academic theologism. That is why the so-called 'sermon on the plain'[36] ends with his distinction between he who 'hears my words and puts them into practice' and he 'who hears my words, and does not put them into practice'. The poor must do something with the news – and accepting it for showcase preservation will not do; that, notably, was a word for both his disciples and the interested periphery.[37]

The bond of word and deed in the hearer was, of course, in the teacher too. As we speak of the centrality of what he said, we must not pull that apart from the testimony of his life and deeds. To heal a servant[38] or to raise a son[39] was as much to spread the news[40] as was the speaking. We have noted that Jesus only spoke in Nazareth of *proclaiming* recovery of sight for the blind, but the fact that he *did* it was telling – and not least in his own mouth. When the doubting John called for reassurance in his cell,[41] that news was itself freedom for the prisoner. To teach John was to proclaim freedom to the prisoner; to teach about him was more, it was to proclaim the year of the Lord's favour, for now in the kingdom even John paled beside each of the poor who had embraced the witness of the king[42] and not closed their minds upon him.

It was a sign of Jesus' love that he kept an eye open for those who were not yet clear whether to open themselves to him or not, and to prise them open when he could. No sooner had Jesus condemned those who shut themselves to him because he ate and drank with anyone,[43] than we find him doing just that with Simon the Pharisee – one of the elite in every sense, in education, religion, social position and wealth. It seems that his invitation mingles courtesy and a genuine desire to understand. He certainly gets more enlightenment than he bargained for, both in Jesus' parable[44] and in the sharp and explicit application which Mark and Matthew both abbreviate.[45]

That teaching was Jesus' habitual activity at this stage is not only Luke's witness ('proclaiming the good news of the kingdom . . . from one town and village to another', for which he gathered a team and needed ongoing material support[46]) it is also the burden of his challenge. The sower parable[47] is rightly preached as testing the response of hearers' hearts to the word of God; yet in Jesus' mouth it was specifically addressed to his *contemporaries*' response to his own prevailing works – that of 'scattering the seed'. Would those who *heard* his word *retain* it? For this reason, relationship with him was defined less by blood than by hearing God's word and putting it into practice.[48]

As Jesus himself was well aware (see the sower) the very octane of his teaching made it difficult to accept. So the disciples battle to learn the lesson of his control over nature[49] and their alarm is repeated in the observers of Legion's deliverance[50] who can hardly wait to get him out of town.[51] Perhaps anticipating just such a reaction, he only allows Jairus, his wife, and three intimates to learn directly from the raising of the dead girl.[52]

The verbal nature of Jesus' work, and its target area in the perceptions of people, is naturally reduplicated in the commission he gives his workers – both the twelve[53] and the seventy-two,[54] so much so that 'he who listens to you listens to me'.[55] It mattered whether people heard and accepted what Jesus had to say. Even the five thousand are fed knowledge first.[56] The seventy-two are sent because the unenlightened are not being taught fast enough, even five thousand at a time.

If learning by doing was one of Jesus' key teaching methods with his followers, the wide group as well as the narrow, 'question and answer' brought out the most central lesson of all, from which moment of revelation the whole mood of the gospel account changes.[57] Peter's confession, reinforced by the revelation at the tranfiguration,[58] begins a period of more solemn and cost-counting teaching in which both mood and content shift. They must learn to carry a cross,[59] to humble themselves,[60] to put Jesus first.[61]

Lawyers,[62] busy housewives,[63] eager disciples,[64] uncertain observers,[65] and forebears of Patience Strong,[66] all receive the enlightenment and correction of the good news; Pharisees and lawyers are taken aback,[67] crowds warned,[68] individuals counselled,[69] disciples encouraged and prepared.[70] Suffering and the sabbath, the kingdom, the way into it, and the role of the king are all covered.[71] He will teach in response to a question or a situation he observes, in direct comment or oblique parabolic challenge, to discourage mindless discipleship,[72] or to encourage the inadequate to respond.[73] Commonsense exhortation[74] alternates with searing social comment.[75] In short, Jesus was a compulsive teacher; whether the hearers flattered him,[76] or were 'confident of their own righteousness and looked down on everybody else',[77] whether they were a town's beggars,[78] or its fat cats,[79] whether the message was in word or dramatic gesture,[80] whether he was proclaiming,[81] prophesying,[82] or pastoring,[83] Jesus longed that his listeners should truly hear: that their lives might be changed by the entrance of his words. That is the teacher, supremely. Luke even portrays his key work after the resurrection as explaining,[84] opening the scriptures,[85] opening their minds[86] and speaking about the kingdom of God.[87]

We have, of course, laboured the point – but for a reason. Sadly there is a need in today's church for an apologia for apologetics. We have to defend the verbal along with the visual and the incarnational announcement of the gospel. Dorcas needs more than preaching, to be sure; but she would be the first to say she was glad for that, and to wish that Alice and Solly should hear it. If some of Fanie's mentors have discredited the business of proclamation by the distortion of its content (and every Christian spokesman has, to some degree, and knows it), that simply justifies Jesus' own approach to similar distortion in his own day – debate, theology, lifestyle, and where necessary, rebuke and hard words. But words, all the same; for the most widespread poor, in Jesus' list of priorities, were clearly those who simply needed to hear and to understand, that they might respond to truth for the sake of life.

The poor sick. It is good that probably the most prominent activity of Jesus which is recorded after his speaking is his work of healing. Nothing is more bluntly physical, more directly bodily, than to be ill or injured; and nothing seems to have aroused his compassion more immediately or consistently than the sight of one afflicted by disease.

I want to leave the vexed question of the demonic for a later section, but the seven or eight instances in Luke need to be borne in mind alongside the crowd of more unequivocally physical cases which he mentions. Nothing could be clearer witness to the sensitivity of Jesus to the immediate bodily needs of man than this area of his ministry, and nothing more quickly rebukes the instinct to spiritualise which has become the ready refuge of many Christians when observable pain of limb or circumstance is staring them in the face.

We have to assume – because of the challenge laid by Jesus in the Nazareth synagogue concerning his activity in Capernaum – that the summary in 4:15 covers a fair amount of healing activity already. After that, and leaving aside the demoniac in 4:31–37, the first recipient of healing at Jesus' hands is Simon Peter's mother-in-law.[88] Here Jesus begins by *rebuking* the fever; this must be either on the view that the treatment appropriate in cases of demon-possession applies, requiring some objective presence of evil lying behind the disease to be banished, or it is simply an expression of divine indignation at the ugliness viciously afflicting God's creatures. This would tie up with the anger expressed by Jesus in the face of leprosy and its consequent ostracism in the alternative (and more likely) reading of Mark 1:41.[89] Luke clearly views the fever as having an existence of its own when he says 'it left her'. No convalescence was needed; indeed there is a hint of healing for a purpose, leading as it did immediately into service of and for Jesus himself.

That this is no isolated instance is immediately underlined by Luke who follows Mark in clearly presenting the early ministry of Jesus as a kind of mass popular movement gathering around the wonder-working preacher.[90] Only a highly significant break for prayer was able to reorientate Jesus to his preaching ministry in the midst of such hectic and dramatically effective activity.[91]

The very next recorded healing of an individual is a leper whose testimony again drew flocks of the sick to Jesus and pressed him into another break for prayer.[92] With the leper, the question of Jesus' perception of the causes and necessary cures of illness begins to arise. We have already seen that some kind of confrontation with evil seems to have been in his mind in dealing with Simon's mother-in-law. With the leper, the pain of the disease lay as much in the required ostracism on grounds of contagion as in the disease itself, debilitating as it was. Assuming for a moment the historicity of miraculous healing power in the work of Jesus, one still wonders how much that miracle was conveyed through the act of long-forgotten touch[93] with all its psychosomatic healing potential.

Jesus' next healing goes further, into what may be called the pneumosomatic; that is, it raises the question of the relation between *spiritual* sickness and physical debility. Here a man is lowered through the roof to Jesus' feet, to whom Jesus declares forgiveness some time before healing his body. Indeed, his response to the unspoken pharisaic question about his authority, 'Which is easier: to say, "Your sins are forgiven", or to say, "Get up and walk"?' is partly to affirm that the easier job of physical healing is but a sign of the deeper work, and partly to affirm that the link between the two is both deeper and more subtle than they have perceived. The suggestion made elsewhere that sin causes disease is here neither made nor excluded; but perhaps the effect in both man and spectators, namely praise to God, was made possible by a release of heart just as much as it was brought on by the wonder of walking again. Poverty was defined by both sickness and sin, or rather, good news was so preached to a whole man that varied areas of his being received freedom at once.[94]

Although much has been made of the so-called 'messianic secret', and the way in which Jesus consequently sought on at least some occasions to minimise the publicity attaching to

his healings, there were several in which precisely the reverse
was the case. Perhaps that was because there was no choice
but to heal in the presence of others; but certainly he was
quick to make object lessons of the situation wherever
possible. Indeed the term 'object lesson' may be too superficial; the healed were not simply illustrations of something
he wanted to say, but were part of that very new creation in
the community which the kingdom of God was. As long as
they remained healed thereafter, they were signs of the
kingdom and emblems of the passing of the king. The lesson
given had become part of their culture, not just a passing
comment. To this extent every individual healed became
part of the healing of the nation, and of the witness to its
hope; perhaps better, the effect of their healings and the
lessons he drew from them demonstrated that they were
never mere individuals to begin with, but part of a whole
creation interlocked in process of redemption. To lift up the
crushed was not just a sign that the year of the Lord's favour
had dawned, though it was that; it was the dawning of
freedom itself.

It is for this reason, the reality that every bondage and
every freedom is interlocked with every other, that so often
the first act of liberation by Jesus drew a string of others in its
train. The paralytic's sin released led through his body
healed to the onlookers' spirits set free in new worship and
the minds of the critics confronted with the possibility of
growth and renewal. Just the same appears in the healing of
the man with the withered hand in the synagogue on the
sabbath.[95] With apparent lack of sensitivity Jesus calls the
man out publicly and before helping him, engages his critics
in debate about healing on the sabbath. He was in fact
confronting an establishment which not only tyrannised the
religious perspectives of the people's minds (a more serious
affliction than our generation acknowledges, but of which
Jesus was most aware); but which so imposed its values on
their lifestyle that God's good recreational gift had become a

slavery and all its connotations negative. All the divinely-intended weekly jubilee-value of the day had been turned into a load with which the rulers burdened the people, doing nothing themselves to help carry it.[96] Until Jesus, no one had had the freedom of perception or the courage of speech to remark the lack of the emperor's clothing in their threadbare but oppressive theology. The man's hand grew dramatically, but not more so than that congregation's shrivelled world-view. Many a church needs a touch of that.

The issue has to arise of exactly what Jesus did it with. Reductionist suggestions that it was all in the mind – so that a little affectionate pat on the head would somehow release the requisite psychosomatic dynamic to do the trick, rather as the feeding of the five thousand was but the sharing of hidden sandwiches when a generous lad but set the needed example – are too thin by far to explain the accounts. Some of the conditions (handicapped limbs or death) are simply not susceptible to that treatment. In some cases the numbers are too great unless one supposes mass suggestibility on an incredible scale.

Luke's own suggestions revolve around the two (and not interchangeable) concepts of power (Greek, *dunamis*) and authority (Greek, *exousia*). They are not the same: the latter is the right to do it, the former the wherewithal, the electricity, the active force. Notably Jesus handed *both* to the twelve[97] – the verse is not a poetic doublet. So as the sermon on the plain opens,[98] the hearers are the great number who have come to hear and to be healed 'because power (*dunamis*) was coming from him and healing them all'.[99] The (notably Gentile) centurion in Capernaum asks Jesus to heal by remote control on the grounds that he himself, as a man under *exousia*, knows authority when he sees it. (To be precise, his comment is that he perceives Jesus also to be *under* it – but that is precisely why he was able to wield it.[100]) Just that authority earns him the soubriquet 'great prophet' when he raises the dead soon afterwards[101] at Nain – though here it is striking that the object of Jesus' compassion, the poor person in his eyes, is not primarily the dead man but his bereaved mother. She counts as the crushed, the broken-hearted of Isaiah. So does John the Baptist when he sends his discouraged enquiry from prison;[102] Jesus' ministry to the sick, and the interpretation he puts on it, are just that sign of the kingdom which accompanies, or maybe is, the very preaching of news to the poor which frees that particular prisoner.

Power and authority are nowhere more neatly interwoven than in the bracketed tale of the dead girl and the woman with the haemorrhage.[103] Invited to deal with the girl, Jesus enters her home and takes control – of the father's fears, of access to the sickbay, of the mourners' mockery, and of the girl herself as he quietly commands her to rise. He then takes charge of the aftercare. Indeed, Luke again implies that authority was needed over something more than her body, for at Jesus' command her spirit returned and – again apparently without gradual recovery or convalescence – she stood up and went back to life as normal. En route to her home, meanwhile, a woman in the crowd touches the hem of Jesus' robe and he immediately perceives that *dunamis*[104] has flowed from his being to heal her. He himself attributes the healing to her faith, fully knowing that it was actually the power that did it; he initiates the complex debate, still in session, over the link between God's power and the recipient's openness in any experience of healing.

As the healing ministry continued, and apparently on a wholesale scale,[105] Jesus continued to use it as a sign of something more, the breaking-in of the kingdom.[106] It also became a focal point of dispute with the synagogue rulers and Pharisees – on two closely related occasions he uses precisely the same argument to demolish their opposition to healing on the sabbath.[107] In the first of these there is again a sideways glance at possible supernormal sources of causation in illness when he refers to the crippled woman in retrospect as 'a daughter of Abraham, whom Satan has kept bound'.[108]

For Jesus, signs of the kingdom were only of value if they bore kingdom fruit. That is, they might point to his kingship, but unless in the process people were led to acknowledge the king and follow him, they were of little worth. For this reason most of the healing accounts either say or strongly hint that the physical healing led on to something more. The last two examples Luke records are explicit on this – the ten lepers of whom only the Samaritan returned to give praise to God in the form of some kind of recognition of Jesus,[109] and blind Bartimaeus (so named by Mark) who 'received his sight and followed Jesus'.[110] Mark is more explicit, using with artistic ambiguity the word for Christian living coined in Acts – 'he followed Jesus in the way'.[111] Recovery of sight for the blind, yes – but in multiple dimensions.

The poor demonised. As we have noted, the relationship between sickness and what the gospels refer to as being 'demonised' is one of a collection of issues in the area of human infirmity, the supernatural, the historicity of miracle and the like which need detailed treatment beyond the scope of this volume. I have listed the demonised separately at this point simply because Luke, for all the overlap which he notes,[112] generally makes a rather clear distinction between the two. In his summaries, the sick and the possessed are distinct categories.[113] In the four instances he gives in lurid technicolour, two have reference to physical conditions which cause scholars to suggest that Luke's diagnosis (or Christ's) may have been merely the product of contemporary medical ignorance. The boy in the valley[114] is commonly referred to as 'epileptic'. His condition is more fully given by Mark;[115] then there is a glancing reference to 'a demon that was mute'.[116] These two could readily be dismissed as physical, nervous or psychological if it were not for the diagnosis given and the treatment brought to bear, which have to be explained away to de-demonise the accounts.

Still more stark are the first account Luke gives us,[117] and the story of Legion.[118] The first is again clearly distinguished from healings which follow; the second may be related to the symptoms of acute psychiatric disturbance. The difficulty with a reductionist description of Legion ('it was *nothing but* a psychological condition . . .') is the suddenness and apparent finality of his healing, the account Jesus himself gave of what was wrong ('Jesus had commanded the evil spirit'), Luke's own interpretation as a medical man, and a good deal of modern exorcism experience which parallels the ministry given to Legion – not to mention, of course, those pigs. All this pushes us back into the realm of our presuppositions, which must be debated more fully elsewhere. Our purpose here is simply to note that whatever these conditions were – and I fully accept that they were multidimensional – Jesus saw the sufferers as part of the poor, and his ministry to them was part of the proclamation of God's good news. Indeed, that news and its acceptance was the guarantee that the sufferers would now move on into freedom and not lapse back into bondage.[119] Just as Bartimaeus' gift of sight was multidimensional, so was the freedom given to this species of captives.

The poor disciples. As we continue to look at the categories of people with whom Jesus dealt, and whom we believe were in his eyes the poor whom he had to evangelise, there is no escaping the fact that he spent an immense proportion of his time trying to enlighten and mature a particular coterie of men whom he had pulled out of professional life to be with him – the disciples. We have seen how the main and central thrust of Jesus' lifetime ministry seems to have been about communication, getting something through to his contemporaries which they desperately needed to grasp. His ministry to his disciples was an intensification of that ministry, training and developing them in detail to be his workers and subsequent representatives. Very often when a casual contact was the apparent object of his attention, he clearly had in mind the effect all this was having on his disciples, and quite often he is seen debriefing the incident with them for their learning. They too had to be freed, given sight and released into the lifestyle of the year of the Lord in order to become his witnesses.

Seen in this way, the healing of Simon's mother-in-law was an act of revelation for Simon Peter himself. So was the discussion about priorities which followed, in which Mark tells us that Peter was the spokesman.[120] So was the fishing expedition whose revelation led straight into both calling and promise.[121] In the condensed account of the gospels, one of the tantalising gaps is the detail of what kind of revelation Levi had experienced before he was able so swiftly to respond to a similar call.[122] The calling of others is hidden until they appear as the twelve, but then immediately they are singled out for instruction – even in the presence of the crowd.[123] They are a set-apart community and they need deeper instruction than the rest; all the second-person address in the so-called 'sermon on the plain' refers to them – *they* are 'you who are poor', 'you who hunger'. The focus must shift shortly after – perhaps this is the significance of the crowd's presence – for it is inconceivable that they could also be 'you who are rich'. It is they who truly 'hear' him[124] and for whom therefore the lifestyle which follows is intended – love of enemy, mercy, generous giving, abstention from criticism, a life built on the implementation of the words of Jesus.[125] It is the same group who have the parable of the sower, and in principle all the parables, explained to them; there is the sharpest distinction between the *you* to whom 'the knowledge of the secrets of the kingdom of God has been given', and the *others* who 'though hearing . . . may not understand'.[126] *They* are his listeners and his lamplighters.[127]

It is just the same when the lessons are drawn from events

more than from didactic teaching. The disciples are the ones in the boat when the storm is calmed,[128] learning from both his action, his rebuke and their own amazed conversation. And when the inner storm of Legion's affliction is also calmed, it is they who constitute 'those who had seen it' and are able to tell the people 'how the demon-possessed man had been cured'.[129]

The training continues with practicals, reviewed with the teacher after exposure to the living ministry environment,[130] rammed home by working alongside him in an apparently impossible task[131] where even a menial involvement taught tangible lessons. Seminar discussion draws out their articulation of their perceptions so that they are both crystallised and corrected.[132]

As the revelation began with Peter, so it goes on in the inner circle of three within the twelve, selected for deeper perception of all Jesus is. Those who have already been with him in the revelation of life at the bedside[133] are also in at the confirmation of Peter's confession on the mountain top.[134]

Nor is the twelve the outer limit – there are moments too when they are rebuked for exclusivism as much as for rivalry,[135] or are deliberately set in the context of a much wider, and also fully instructed team[136] – but even then it is the disciples who are *privately* told not to miss the special quality of what they are experiencing in their day. There is again a delicious ambiguity in the precise weight of the words, 'Blessed are the eyes that see what you see': the blind are receiving their sight.

Being in his confidence, the disciples are used to being with Jesus at prayer[137] so they have the opportunity (and evidently the freedom in themselves) to make enquiries about it, which are met.[138] They are *first* (in what sense?) to be given some of his warnings[139] even when a crowd appears to be present; they are the recipients of ongoing lifestyle teaching;[140] they are themselves at times unclear whether his

words are addressed 'to us, or to everyone'.[141] Certainly they
are not exempt from that wider teaching which *is* for
everyone.[142] They are those who can be entrusted with
his word because they have accepted God's invitation to
dinner,[143] taken up his emblem,[144] and have been found and
rehabilitated by his initiative.[145] Having known such grace,
they can only live by a higher standard;[146] they must indeed
'watch' themselves, both in conduct and in gullibility in the
face of false teaching.[147] They are the ones called to
persistent prayer,[148] they are taken aside and given the
prophetic word[149] even when they, with all their inside
knowledge, cannot grasp it. In Jerusalem, they find the
donkey and fix the supper; at it, they are his guests.[150] When
they pass comment about the buildings, the moment is
taken for Christ's excursus on the near and distant future
on which they have to set their sights;[151] these insights are
not for the wider crowd who continue to press in on Christ's
attention.[152]

It is John who superbly prefixes the last supper with his
comment that Jesus 'Having loved his own who were in the
world', 'loved them to the end', or 'showed them the full
extent of his love'.[153] Luke likewise sees this as an exclusive
time in which not only the twelve, but several individuals
within the group, receive special attention – notably Peter,
John and Judas. They are taught, warned, washed and fed.[154]
The inner trio of Peter, James and John are again together in
the garden; Judas is challenged in the garden[155] and even
Peter – by a glance – by the fireside.[156]

It is well enough known that only one of the resurrection
appearances of Jesus is to a non-disciple (that to his natural
brother James) but the circle may be wider than the twelve –
though not much, judging from the way Cleopas and his
companion know how to rush back to the upper room – but
throughout it is his own followers who are taught and
encouraged, challenged and recommissioned during those
weeks.[157]

The point is obvious enough. When Jesus preached his good news to the poor, he included in that the intensive training of a little band of followers. What they did with that training we shall see in chapter six. The point here is simply to undermine any simplistic account of Jesus' ministry which sees it as a healing campaign, a preaching mission, or an embryonic social revolution in isolation. The teaching given to these men was not only deeper but far more wide ranging and complex than any of those things alone. It was the preparation for – and in a nutshell it was – what the Lausanne Covenant has called 'the whole gospel for the whole man in the whole world.'

The poor sinners. One of the greatest embarrassments to a narrowly liberationist presentation of the gospels is Jesus' apparent obsession with forgiveness. As the Pharisees rightly perceived, none but God can forgive sins; there is simply no humanist interpretation of any passage which deals with the subject. It is overtly and unavoidably supernaturalist; it deals with man's connections with God. There is no way of making sense of Jesus which excludes the thought that when he released the prisoner and the oppressed, this dimension of moral bondage and spiritual imprisonment was in his mind – though not to the exclusion of more concrete connotations.

Luke 5 illustrates this. The Pharisees in question were present when the paralytic was lowered through the roof, and before healing him – which he did not omit to do, since bodies matter to Jesus – Jesus insisted on declaring him forgiven in the sight of God. The man went home praising God; all he needed, for that time anyway, had been done.[158] It is no accident, I suspect, that the next figure who appears is Levi;[159] when Jesus meets his friends, the Pharisees essentially pick up the same issue as before – for Jesus to consort with them is to express an implicit forgiveness for the way they are, which cut across the Pharisees' presuppositions. When Jesus responds, that is precisely the point he makes – 'I have . . . come to call . . . sinners'.

The poor Pharisees are again in the firing line the next time real sinners appear – this time at the dinner table, when the sinful woman made such an exhibition of herself all over Jesus' feet.[160] Her sensuous response to him is, in his eyes, a sign of that inner release which has given self-respect back to the despised, new hope and cleanliness to the sordid. Only Luke records so fully the extent of Jesus' verbal demolition of Simon's proper but restrained response to himself. We recall that in Luke 4:18 it was not only that *freedom* was expressed in the basic word for forgiveness, but *release* which had connotations of jubilant dance on entering into sunshine after years in the cell; that was precisely the woman's style. She may be excluded from Simon's table, but the great banquet was spread for the likes of her.[161] Because we read parables in isolation, we readily lose sight of the polemical context in which they were first used, and the controversial purpose to which they were first put. The triad of parables about the lost in Luke 15 – the sheep, the coin, the son – were actually a sustained defence of Jesus' ministry among the lost in the face of criticism from the Pharisees and teachers of the law. Although the term 'sinner' in the first century connoted not only moral wrong but the common people of the land upon whom the elite looked down their noses, it clearly also carried that moral sense. Each parable refers to the bringing back by Jesus of people who had become out of touch with God. The clearest, of course, is the son whose forgiveness and restoration is explicit – and the elder brother, depicted in all his meanness, is an insulting image of Jesus' very critics themselves. They not only needed forgiveness themselves and couldn't see it; they could not bring themselves to rejoice at one sinner who repented, nor to encourage one shepherd who sought him out.

Perhaps the most lively prodigal in Luke (who, like the parable, would be unknown to us but for Luke) is the despised Zacchaeus in his tree.[162] He fits the parable so neatly because Jesus describes his ministry to Zacchaeus exactly as seeking and saving the lost.[163] As with the sinful woman, it is not his action which earns his salvation; his action is the symptom and emblem of something deeper going on – from man's side repentance, from God's forgiveness.

It is Matthew rather than Luke who quotes Jesus' words of institution at the last supper with a specific reference to forgiveness,[164] though Luke's 'poured out *for you*' in the context carried the same meaning; the passover context and the talk of a new covenant would suggest release in its widest reference. That is how Luke sees the cross which the supper foreshadowed; he stresses the innocence of Jesus, refers to Barabbas who is released indirectly through Jesus' death (though with a less direct hint of substitutionary doctrine than Matthew), and alone records the gracious promise of paradise to the dying thief – undoubtedly meant as a proclamation of forgiveness. As the risen Jesus then looks forward to his followers' work, it is that 'repentance and forgiveness of sins will be preached in his name to all nations'[165] – clearly carrying forward his own commission to preach release to the poor.

The poor unjust. Having ruled out a narrowly liberationist view of Jesus' work, it might be good at this point to tackle head-on that part of Jesus' ministry which the more 'spiritual' Christians like to overlook, and to see those areas in which Jesus did exercise a ministry of very practical release for the poor. To do so I want to start at the other end – to show how much of what he did for the poor, oppressed and needy was a result of what he had to say to, or to do for, the unjust, the rich and the powerful. Those three terms largely refer to the same kinds of people, but we may see more clearly if we take them one at a time for emphasis.

Everyone knows that the epitome of injustice in first-century Israel was the taxman. Unrestrained by exact limits on what he was to collect, he obtained a licence from the Roman occupiers and had to hand over to them a fixed amount. He was then able to count on their patronage to extract that amount from the people of a given area, or from the traders who passed through (it is striking that the two gospel examples were based in centres on the trade routes – Levi in Capernaum and Zacchaeus in Jericho).

When Jesus called Levi,[166] he 'left everything'. That is tantalisingly little to be told; did he simply leave home and travel with Jesus? Or did he resign his tax licence and sell the booth? Did he anticipate the reaction of Zacchaeus and rectify as many of his injustices as he could? All we know for certain is that he laid on a feast for his friends – all of them contemptible in the eyes of the Pharisees. They may have been the poor in one sense, but by definition those he exploited were not helped by that hospitality – they were far from his friends. Yet clearly material generosity and evangelistic zeal (for the purpose of the dinner was that they meet Jesus) went hand in hand. He did, however, renounce his lifestyle in the act of becoming a disciple and then an apostle, being now committed to proclaiming that neighbour-love which cancelled his previous business principles. There must have been implications for his wealth in being despatched for mission without bread, bag, tunic or money; did he leave a pile in the bank so that his apostolic lifestyle was merely play-acting; or did the apostolic band truly have nowhere to lay their heads – with no Capernaum retirement home when their ministry was over? The radical nature of Jesus' call to them, and the blunt 'follow' to Levi, would be largely discredited if nothing dramatic happened to the loot in his Capernaum account. If only we knew.

With Zacchaeus, we do know[167] – but we often miss the point. Apart from the distracting Sunday-school emphasis on climbing trees and having Jesus to tea, the best most of us do is to see him as another individual example of the seeking and saving ministry of Jesus. There are, though, some further dimensions. It is only when Zacchaeus has announced his plan of restitution that Jesus declares 'salvation has come to this house'; and while that may be his comment on the fruit of repentance already evident in Zacchaeus' life, it should further make us ask what salvation consists of. Is it just individual responses to Jesus, maybe evidenced by acts of restitution and generosity; or is it a wider reality of God's work in the world, in which not only individuals are saved but other scars on God's order are healed – in which, in other words, the Old Testament's image is fulfilled of a world in which God is Lord and his people dwell at peace with him and each other, in a shalom of true worship, social harmony, justice and compassion? Isaiah would surely have expected *all* these symptoms to be present in the setting of God's salvation. This being so, it is striking that Zacchaeus offered to do two things, not one; his 'Here and now I give . . . to the poor, and if I have cheated . . . I will pay back' is not a kind of Jewish poetic doublet, an effusive repetition for effect. It is a renewed commitment to *two* standards in the law and the prophets, namely compassion *and* justice. That is, the law commanded and expected consideration for the widows, the fatherless, the aliens and the needy; giving half his possessions to the poor was a response to that. But restoring what he had stolen was a response to that part of the law which forbade exploitation, theft, usury, misuse of legal procedure and the abuse of force. Here Jesus was utterly at one with his cousin's advice to the taxmen, interestingly bracketed with the command to soldiers not to extort money.[168] The distinction may be fine, but it is real; the law forbade both the making of paupers, and the neglect of existing ones. One has to speculate about the effect on a community the size of Jericho, but it must have been considerable: anyone who can afford to give away half he has and still refund an array of defrauded clients is well-heeled, and the release of resources on that scale can have been little less than a social revolution in the town. It will not do, then, to work for Alice Barrington's salvation only in terms of what it does for her in securing eternal life, nor even to greet a new generosity on her part as a useful by-product of her conversion. She is not an island but part of a social complex; for her to come to Christ *has* to mean the release of some of her assets as a fruit of repentance, and that release itself is no incidental but is integral to the reality of salvation for both the plan of God and for his world, which far transcends the conversion of individual souls.

This is precisely the point made in the parable of the rich man and Lazarus,[169] one of the most vivid and scathing Jesus ever told. The picture of the rich man in purple and the near-corpse at his gate, too weak even to shoo off the street-scavenging dogs, is well enough known, but again the punchline is often missed. When 'Dives' pleads with Abraham to send warning to his brothers who share his lifestyle and attitudes, the response is 'If they do not listen to Moses and the Prophets, they will not be convinced even if someone rises from the dead.' The thrust of this appears if we ask, what exactly was Dives' sin for which he was condemned to perdition? It was simply that though he thought himself a good Jew, he had wholly disregarded the law of Moses and the exhortations of the prophets; and no further evidence of that was needed than his treatment of Lazarus. Had he listened to the scriptures of his people, he would have seen that his neglect of this man was – as with Zacchaeus – a violation of both justice and compassion. It was not permitted so to order society that a man be reduced to that condition; and when it happened by the fecklessness of a man himself, it was still not permitted to neglect his basic needs. To love one's neighbour *as oneself* was not an innovation of Jesus; even the measure – 'as yourself' – was written into the law,[170] and that standard summed up the whole law and the prophets. For Dives to be a Jew – a child of Abraham, the very accolade afforded the converted Zacchaeus – was for him to raise Lazarus' standard of living to the level of his own, purple, fine linen, and all. Or at least it was so to modify that lifestyle that more than what fell from the table would be available to his neighbour. It had to be sufficient for his basic human needs.

To say that the great commandment required total financial equality would be saying too much; Old Testament expectations at their highest did not say that. But to say that the law's intention, with the device of the jubilee and the sharp eye of the prophets reinforcing it, was to ensure a broad band of togetherness in lifestyle where wealth was neither excessive nor entrenched and abject poverty was ruled out, is sure. The unjust had enough trouble in accepting that these standards were their responsibility in Israel: Jesus' good Samaritan was meant to assert that they were global. It arose, after all, from a question over the interpretation of that very commandment.

It is for this reason – that those best able to exploit were also those best educated and able to know the law – that Jesus' strictures on the Pharisees were so fiercely social. They should have lived out Moses' law to the poor in exemplary ways: yet they 'neglect justice',[171] calming their conscience by detailed fulfilment of ceremonial law to the point of weighing out tithes of kitchen herbs. Such myopia is doubly blameworthy, when law advocated conceals law ignored. Injustice is reinforced when the oppressor lays a heavy weight of legal observance on the very ones who suffer from the law's distortion.[172]

The poor powerful. It should not be thought – as is often said – that Jesus challenged the scribes and lawyers because they were religious leaders who were therefore 'in his province', but abstained from challenging those in other roles whom to criticise might seem 'political comment'. That is anyway too narrow an understanding of the role of the Pharisees and Sadducees, who were highly political. But anyhow the distinction does not hold up. Herod was no religious leader, and his injustice – trying to kill Jesus, and later making light of his dignity and his need for protection at law – received scathing words and a no less scathing silence.[173] Nor is it true that Jesus only addressed Jewish injustice; his comment to Pilate in John 19:11, 'You would have no power over me if it were not given to you from above', entirely fits the less explicit challenge to Pilate to use his power justly which Jesus presents in all the gospels. Indeed, Jesus' second temptation – to use power unjustly himself – is the basis of a consistent theme in his ministry, a standing challenge to all holders of power or authority to use it as to God or risk its decline into self-aggrandisement or ruthless exploitation. He would have the powerful released from their own injustice as much as he would have the powerless released from its effects. The crucifixion must stand for ever as the ultimate rebuke to injustice, to the devious use of power, to the lie, to kangaroo courts and pliable magistrates, to torture and chicanery and the cheapening of human life, to legal expediency and the bureaucratic shrug.

Jesus' own protest at injustice flared out most vividly in the temple, when he found those who 'devour widows' houses'[174] setting up in the house of God to devour the resources of the poor worshippers with a system of short-change mercenary religion. Here there was no means of appeal and the power of the system simply ripped off the poor for the spare fat of the leaders' lifestyle. But it was more than that; the words Jesus chose, 'you have made it "a den of robbers"', were a reference to days when previously the temple had fallen into sin, and then too it was not only false religion but social injustice which prevailed.[175] The market in the temple symbolised their wider need to 'really change your ways and your actions and deal with each other justly . . . not oppress the alien, the fatherless or the widow . . . not shed innocent blood'.[176]

It was, of course, the response of the leaders to this protest which led Jesus to warn his followers of the unjust persecution they were likely to experience; even his death and resurrection would not stop the coming with swords and clubs[177] which his cause and its adherents would have to face. So he warned them to be ready for hands to seize them and drag them before synagogues, kings and governors, to fling them into prison. So too, he was proclaiming release to the captives in preparing them to handle injustice as much as in the promise that it would all one day be done away with.

The poor rich. Apart from Levi, Zacchaeus and Dives, the rich make a number of other appearances in Luke.

As we have seen, the Pharisees were not just attacked for their religious error. They 'loved money', and sneered at Jesus' contention that they could not be loyal to it and to God at the same time.[178] He proved his point over pharisaic dinner tables.[179] At the first he challenged his host over the loveless heart which accompanied his comfortable conventions. At the second he climbed into their double standards, as much over justice and love as over overtly 'religious' obligations.[180] At the third he challenged both the social climb syndrome and the tit-for-tat entertaining system which prevails in affluent communities everywhere:[181] the families of Alice, Solly and Fanie would all find it novel to 'invite the poor, the crippled, the lame, the blind'. So far have our social conventions been Christianised!

Nowhere is the grip of mammon tighter than in the disposal of an estate, and it is that situation which provokes the telling of the sharp little parable of the rich fool.[182] The point is again that to be 'rich towards God' is not often compatible with material wealth, let alone with ambitious business development plans; 'I will build' can be the highway to folly. This is why the parable of the banquet with which Jesus followed up his challenge to the social customs of the Pharisees is not a change of direction, confronting them in vague general terms about their response to the kingdom of God;[183] it precisely puts its finger on property and business as two – and possibly the details of a marriage settlement as the third – of man's most common excuses for disobedience. Those were the Pharisees' problems, and it is no accident that the cost of discipleship occupies the following verses.[184]

That very reluctance is the problem of the young ruler 'of great wealth' whose interview with Jesus provokes the Lord's discourse on the difficulty affluence always affords to discipleship.[185] Whether the needle's eye was literal, or a colloquialism for the small doors cut in Jewish gateways for use at night, the image of the overloaded camel is vivid enough: those with most baggage have most trouble getting through. Hermeneutics have worked hard to soften the thrust of Jesus' words to the man himself ('sell everything . . .') arguing that this was an individual whose personal problem cannot be universalised as a challenge to all potential disciples; Jesus was perceiving *his* need, we say, but thank goodness we don't all have to buy that remedy in order to be Christians. There would, of course, be howls of horror if we said the same of Nicodemus, whose individual need was to be born from above, or of Peter, who was called to follow; those are surely universals. So what is the difference when the remedy was in each case prescribed in an identical context of individual counsel? Perhaps we had better exegete some of these other encounters a little less automatically; but maybe too we need to see the universal challenge implicit in this encounter. After all, Jesus immediately universalises it to say that money forms a block to discipleship. I suspect that attitudes to the acquiring, holding and using of it should much more often be topics for repentance and find more place in evangelistic preaching, than they do; Bridleway Baptist please note. Indeed, the very rationalising of the rich ruler's encounter may have much to do with the individualising and spiritualising which goes on in gospel preaching, and much to do as a result with the emaciated kingdom which often gets introduced as a result. We simply do not show the way to the kingdom in its fullness, and fail most often at the point of evangelism – no wonder, then, that those with social or humane priorities are suspicious of evangelism at all. Emmanuel Presby may be shut in to a partial gospel but its perception of Bridleway and Corybantic as shut in too is totally correct. When those who view the world through the left eye and refuse to open the right insist that their vision is true, those who see only through the right can be excused a certain reluctance to open both. We are often so shocked at the words 'sell everything' that we miss the purpose of the sale, which is to 'give to the poor'; the challenge of Jesus to this man was not only to release himself from the bondage of mammon, but to release others from the grip of need. That – the building of the kingdom in a wide sense, and the willingness to sacrifice for it – guaranteed 'treasure in heaven'.

The ruler's bondage of heart is contrasted with the freedom shown by the widow with her offering in the temple,[186] who again is contrasted with the rich who can afford to appear generous without actually opening their hearts at all. Because these very people devour widows' houses, the Old Testament's view is underlined – the poor and oppressed are so often the imitators and lovers of God, the rich and powerful battle to stay near him because of what it costs them, in actions and business procedures as much as in cash. For this reason the Lucan beatitudes hit the nail on the head; the poor are undefined as to whether their poverty is of spirit or of pocket-book, but the two overlap so much that the promise of the kingdom is really what defines them: the poor in spirit will inherit it by faith, and the poor in body are the likeliest catchment area for the poor in spirit. As for the rich, they need only be defined materially, for we know that in spirit they must always negotiate the needle's eye to qualify – and must shed some baggage en route to prove the fruits of their repentance. Dorcas does not qualify automatically, for salvation is not by poverty, but by grace through

faith; she does, though, sit at the place where to appropriate
that grace is not hard. Alice, by contrast, may not (despite
some evangelicals) qualify through a change of heart alone,
for her change of heart can only be real when evidenced in
turning from the actualities of a life of acquisitive sin. As
Calvin has it, 'salvation is by faith alone, but saving faith is
never alone'. Those who are well fed now – a term clearly
expanding what is meant above it by the rich – can only pass
through the needle's eye in fellowship with those who hunger
now, and in such fellowship that they lovingly serve them
into health. It is not likely that the world will speak well of
those who rock the social boat in this way; indeed the bond
between wealth and power will ensure that the power is used
to exclude and persecute those who are, here and now as
much as there and then, inheriting the kingdom.[187]

Lest this appear to be sliding into a wholesale rejection of
property and possessions when held by Christian people, it
must be said that Jesus also teaches a positive obverse side to
the matter. The widow is not commended because her gift
shows how released she is from the grip of wealth, at least not
only for that. It is also because of the end to which she gives
it, namely the work of God; and it was not wrong in principle
for the temple to receive it, though Jesus might have had his
criticisms if he had reviewed the expenditure column in that
particular year's temple management accounts. He sees no
wrong in material resources, which are anyway essentially
temporary in nature, being used for the eternal purposes of
God. That is the thrust of the often-misunderstood parable of
the shrewd manager,[188] where a blatantly caricatured figure
who has engaged in fraud is commended by Jesus not for
fraud but for sagacity in his situation. The conclusion Jesus
draws is that his followers should deploy their worldly goods
to 'gain friends for yoursel(ves), so that when it is gone, you
will be welcomed into eternal dwellings'. The conventional
evangelical interpretation of that verse is that Christians
should so place their funds in evangelism that the fruits of

that endeavour are converted people who will welcome the donor in due time at the gates of heaven. There is some validity in that, not least because Jesus' reference to the eternal dwellings rules out a this-world-only perspective. But does 'gain friends' bear only that interpretation? Could it not as much be the kind of thing Zacchaeus was doing, signifying the arrival of the kingdom precisely by relieving the poverty and injustice around him, and especially those parts of it which he had himself created? If that is part of the work of the kingdom, will it not evoke a welcome into the dwellings of the God of justice as much as the support of evangelism? This is not to say either that he who gave materially in this way earnt his entry into the eternal dwellings by his actions, or that those who benefited would qualify for those dwellings.. He needs to appropriate grace for himself, and so do they. But surely that is not what this parable is about: it is about the fruits of salvation which ought to be evident in the lives of those who have appropriated grace already, and are as such set free from the grip of possessions to make them free in a practical manner for the work of God through which his kingdom will be built – both evangelism and the relief of suffering. This parable is not about Dorcas and Alice so much as about which of their local churches is doing the job of God towards them; which is releasing resources which will lead to the salvation of both of them, through the sharing of the news of Jesus and the practical alleviation of conditions which dehumanise God's creatures and are an abomination in his loving eyes. The link of material and spiritual is tighter still – he who uses well his little may be given greater responsibility in the kingdom, and even he who does well with the material may be promoted to handle the spiritual. They are not in conflict when both are subservient to the purposes of the king.[189]

The poor poor. If the poor should gain by how Jesus deals with the rich, and the oppressed find release through his word to the powerful, what is the more direct ministry which Jesus directed to the underdog in his own life? They will, of course, benefit from the new lifestyle adopted by all his followers; one cannot 'give to everyone who asks you' or lend to enemies without someone receiving what is given.[190] If the poor and the lame start attending banquets there begins a nutritional revolution. When the ordinary disciples start doing what the one rich client was invited to do, selling their possessions and giving to the poor,[191] then the church of Acts 2 and 4 begins to reappear. Some of the lost sons who return need more than a Bible and a place in a pew; they may need a robe or shoes or a meal, if not prize veal. As the Dives class hears the voice of Abraham through the voice of Jesus through the voice of his people, whether in India, South America, Africa or the West, so an array of hopeless Dorcases and Lazaruses will be rehabilitated, and their sons will never reach the pavement in the first place. The Zacchaeuses of the world can still transform the Jerichos of the world, and the teachers of the law can get their sticky fingers off the widows' houses. So much by itself is revolutionary. But did Jesus not change things directly too?

The poor hungry. It is probably in the twin fields of food and health that the direct impact of Jesus on the physical conditions of the poor was most marked. While knowing that man needed more than a grubstake,[192] the other gospels are explicit that Jesus' compassion was provoked by physical hunger in itself. Matthew has him express the concern that 'these people . . . may collapse'.[193] Mark deliberately juxtaposes the five thousand whom he cares about because they need teaching[194] – and who receive a double nutrition – and the four thousand who evoke his compassion because, simply, 'they . . . have nothing to eat'.[195] That is sufficient mandate for every Christian feeding programme and every agricultural training project on the face of the planet. The feedings were, as John makes clear, signs of something more than a concern for food; indeed he records Jesus running away from a crowd who understandably wanted to make such a useful economist king, and later challenging those same people for their mercenary materialism.[196] He was himself the bread for whom they should seek; and while that thrust justifies those who evangelise in order that inner food reaches the soul of man, it cannot undo the act of feeding which was by its very compassion a sign of the presence of the king. And while it might be naughty to put the changing of the water into wine – itself a sign of something more – into a bracket with the matter of food, it also bespeaks at one level a loving and practical concern with the things of everyday life which may be needed – or even just wanted – by ordinary people. Although Luke has compressed the account of the five thousand[197] his medic's eye does not omit to note that they ate *until satisfied*; a theology of nutrition is hiding here somewhere. Interestingly Dives and Lazarus are introduced largely in terms of food, and not only the lack of it on the pavement; God's challenge is to the obesity of the few as much as towards the basic needs of the many. If Alice starts running soup to Dorcas, that does not of itself justify her dinner parties.

We have already dealt with the large section of his time and energy which Jesus devoted to the sick. We could here add that although some of these were the offspring of rulers and centurions, the bulk appear to have been from the poorer sections of the community. That is no surprise, for disease comes not only from bacteria and viruses but from malnutrition and its resulting vulnerability. Jesus' concern for the sick was in this way part of his concern for the hungry and vice versa; Luke the preventive physician spotted that. It speaks as much to Emmanuel Presbyterian in their use of funds as it does to Corybantic Chapel in theirs.

The poor mourners. There remain some other categories of deprivation and need among men, even when one has explored both the overtly spiritual and the bluntly social parts of Jesus' work – some of the poor whom he embraced and whom we have yet to include. Among the most touching are the bereaved, who – for all the term's wider connotations – must be included in 'Blessed are you who weep now'.[198] Luke alone gives us the account of the widow of Nain, a village just across the valley from Nazareth, to whom (rather than to her dead son) Jesus' heart went out.[199] No doubt this was straightforwardly because of her grief for her son; but Luke, in pointing out that he was her *only* son, may well be hinting at the ultimate tragedy in a primal society, the loss of the breadwinner and the only security for one's old age. She was poor indeed; and was made truly rich when Jesus not only raised the son from death, but 'gave him back to his mother'.

The other mourners in the gospel are those who mourn for Jesus himself – the women en route to the cross whom he gently pauses to counsel,[200] and the disciples after his death. Strikingly both those on the road and those left in town receive the same encouragement: his presence and his teaching.[201] That is enough to lift the gloom.

The poor persecuted. Interestingly it is that same combination – presence and explanation – which Jesus uses to comfort and prepare another group for whom he cared, those who would suffer opposition for his name: those whom 'men hate . . . exclude . . . insult . . . reject'.[202] Luke is at one with John in the emphasis in the farewell discourses on the blessing of being prepared in advance; they would suffer, but must plan ahead to make no response save that given in the moment of trial through the presence of Jesus with them,[203] a presence assured by the reality of the Spirit.[204]

The poor harassed. It is not only the great persecutions of world history which make stress which some find hard to bear. It seems a little matter, but there is an all-too-relevant homeliness in the way Jesus notices those whose poverty is that of anxiety, fretfulness and workaholic strain. Solly Menachemson is not far away. Martha is the obvious case, distracted (literally and vividly, 'dragged off') by all her frantic hostessing. Dr Luke was a sharp psychologist too – his word for her preparations is *diakonia*, our term for Christian ministry – one of the world's most workaholic industries.[205] She has to learn a sense of proportion between the quite valid activity of her life, and its more reflective counter-part. (I write carefully: no man who has ever been taken to task by his women's group over 'you men and your flaming Mary, how do you think the work ever gets done?' would tread unwisely in this exegesis . . .) Martha is not, of course, an isolated example; if she were, the glory of Jesus' teaching on worry[206] and probably his guidance over the end times,[207] would never have been given. Both daily stress and the special hassles of discipleship drew his compassionate attention.

The poor women. Martha puts us on the trail of another group of the poor, one whose situation in many ways has been least revolutionised since Jesus' day – the women. It is common-place to say that Jesus afforded women an immense dignity quite unheard of in his day; for us it is difficult to sense just how much of a jolt that was, even when we have not incorporated his attitude significantly into the life of today's church.

Just list the examples. Simon's mother-in-law, not only healed but given (quite explicitly) a ministry, perhaps one not usually open to women (see p. 100). The widow of Nain (p. 125) and the sinful woman at the Pharisee's dinner (p. 111). He healed them, delivered them from spirits, and was willing to accept their support.[208] And there is his own mother,[209] a girl of twelve and a haemorrhaging woman who would never have dreamt of emerging from anonymity unless he had drawn her into public view to express love to her.[210] Martha and Mary (both received his ministry), a cripple,[211] the mourners of Jerusalem, and supremely the women at the tomb[212] – who else of Jewish men would ever have let that happen?! He noticed women where others would have ignored them – the haemorrhage as well as the widow with her mite – and every bit of his teaching on divorce was designed to wake up callous men to the assumptions on which their arrogant attitude to women was based. Even his response to the Sadducees' idiotic question about marriage in heaven[213] breathes indignation at their fatuous way of thinking about the overworked girl herself. Much of it is hints and attitudes more than anything said; but taken as a whole it is a pervasive testimony to an approach to people, a symptom of release for the imprisoned and freedom for the oppressed.

The poor children. With their contempt for women, it was not surprising that Jesus' society was equally impatient with children; but again he would not join in. When the disciples become irascible with them, he rebukes them and gives time to the children;[214] he uses a child as a model of the man,[215] and gives quite a proportion of his healing ministry to them. Children are seen and heard when he is about.

The poor Gentiles. Two categories of people, both of major theological significance, remain. Jesus provoked the Nazareth congregation more than anything by his own fierce allegiance to Isaiah's global vision, his refusal to be boxed by the possessive nationalistic totemism which bedevilled Jewish history and upset so many of the prophets. His allusions to Naaman and the widow of Zarephath were a declaration of intent; while tactics might require him to begin with the house of Israel and leave the wider circle to his followers, the strategy was defiantly to include them – and some of them were touched in his own ministry as a declaration of that intent. His thrust to the ends of the earth, laid on the church (see p. 145), was implicit in his concept of the poor from the outset. They were, after all, those who needed the activity of God on their behalf; and to the true Jewish mind, none could have that need more than the poor Gentiles.

So it is that Jesus not only heals the servant of a centurion (by definition a Roman) but holds up his faith as an exemplary contrast with the response of his own countrymen.[216] Whether Legion lived among the Gerasenes, Gadarenes or Gergasenes (the manuscripts differ), it had to be all-Gentile territory – how else a large herd of pigs? This was, then, across the lake to the east, beyond Hebrew Galilee;[217] that adds point to the local inhabitants' inability to make sense of Jesus, and their desire to be rid of him.

It is most likely that the sign of Jonah[218] is not, as often thought, to do with the resurrection; neither the book of Jonah itself nor Jesus' comments about it focus that much on the fish, whose three-day incarceration of the prophet could foreshadow the tomb of Jesus. The emphasis of Jonah is on proclamation to the Gentiles – the whole point of the book is to challenge the narrow Jewish nationalism which would run away from a calling to Gentile Nineveh and then sulk in case God granted Gentiles such repentance as to be delivered from judgement. And that is precisely the part Jesus hits on: '*as* Jonah was a sign to the Ninevites, *so* will the Son of Man be . . .' The Queen of Sheba will join the Ninevites in pointing the finger of judgement at Jesus' generation because she too took the trouble as a Gentile to explore the truth to be found in Israel, whereas his own received him not when he came. A point to note here is that, while we think of Matthew as the gospel which brings up the Old Testament scriptural guns to reinforce Jesus' place and teaching, most of Luke's direct citations from it are on this one point – to demonstrate that scripture itself supports the unpopular commitment of Jesus' ministry to include the Gentiles.

A further hint may be found in the parable of the great

banquet.[219] While one must always guard against allegorising the parables, there may well be significance in the double ending of the story; it is not just that the excuses of the privileged (the religious Jews) lead to a closing of the door against them and the inclusion of the poor and blind in their place; when 'there is still room', a second mission follows to the country lanes. Are the poor of the city, the despised in Israel, and those beyond in the countryside the Gentiles? Many interpreters believe so.

If such a thrust is there in Luke 14, maybe we should ask if it is also implied in the great parables of the lost in chapter 15; if they are polemical pieces designed to challenge pharisaic objections to a ministry to the outsider, who is more lost than the Gentile? Perhaps not the sheep, which would symbolically be part of the Jewish flock,[220] nor even the coin from a specifically Jewish wedding headdress. But the son? If he could wander into Gentile territory as he did (pigs again), is it so impossible that he could have brought his employer home with him – and that he too would have been welcome? Certainly some such polemic lies in the bluntest of all parables, that of the tenants in the vineyard;[221] here Jesus not only demolishes the present tenants, the leaders of the nation, but asserts that part of the judgement will be that the owner *will give the vineyard to others*. No wonder his hearers gasped, 'May this never be!'

It is then no surprise in the Lucan version of the commission of the risen Jesus to his church to find that they are commanded to proclaim the good news of repentance and forgiveness in Jesus' name to all nations. Sure they must begin at Jerusalem, but there is no end.[222] Acts spells it out, but it was there all along – and a large part of why he was crucified.

The poor halfbreeds. No less significant is what Jesus has to say, and what he does in relation to the Samaritans. They are, of course, a special case in the New Testament. Their forebears having been exiled by the Assyrians, whose deliberate policy of geographical fragmentation and racial admixture was as effective an antidote to ethnic resistance as any of the world's conquerors has yet found, they were a mixed-blood community set between Judea and Galilee whom Jews found singularly repugnant; the two races had the fetching habit of spitting at each other on sight. Jesus' attitude to them was not only an affront to the racism of his people; it was an affirmation of the dignity of man in the face of all kinds of ethnic prejudice everywhere.

John, of course, clearly highlights the attitude of Jesus here with his choice of travel route through Samaria[223] when many Jews would have taken the far longer way of crossing the Jordan into fully Gentile territory and crossing back again if they wanted to get from Judea to Galilee – such are the absurdities of separation (Fanie please note); he also gives us the woman at the well and the transformation of her whole community (with whom Jesus was not afraid to stay the night).[224] But Luke makes the same points: Jesus passes through Samaria[225] and has to challenge the all-too-typical response of his disciples, whose thoughts of fire from heaven make them the patron saints of the modern racial terror-bomber. They must have squirmed when Jesus framed the parable of the good Samaritan to illustrate the boundaries of neighbour-love;[226] indeed the position of it in the gospel suggests that the trip through Samaria might well have occasioned that piece of artistry in the mind of the Lord. No more eloquent assertion of cross-racial responsibility has entered the world's literature – and Jesus lives it out.

Luke alone preserves for us the account of the ten lepers[227] and highlights the fact that the only grateful one was a Samaritan; so that although the use of that story in the church usually has to do with the churlish lack of gratitude among Christians for what God has done for them, that was by no means its original thrust – which was, as with the centurion, to show that Jesus often received a more open response from foreigners than from his fellow countrymen, and so to reinforce the case for a global Christian mission. Precisely because they were the unfree, the unwanted, the hostile, Jesus wanted to preach good news to them – and they found a special place in his commission to his church[228] for that very reason. Their inclusion in the church, like that of the Gentiles, would signify everything about the identity of the poor and their destiny in Christ – but that is still a little ahead (see p. 145). For now we simply see the force with which Jesus defended his ministry among yet another unexpected and unwanted group, and his determination to cast his ministry as widely as he possibly could.

5   PRIORITIES PREACHED

In reviewing the activity of Jesus we have unavoidably touched on a good deal of his teaching; here we pick up some missing pieces.

The blessings and the woes

What we know under the form of Matthew's gospel as 'the sermon on the mount' is a block of teaching on the nature and conditions of discipleship which finds itself spread around through Luke's gospel.

Obviously we must pay attention to Luke's version of the beatitudes[1] and the relationship between them and Matthew's rendering. But first we need to appreciate their setting in a section of Luke largely devoted to the radical nature of the ministry of Jesus and his calling to his followers. He has just responded to a fairly minor enquiry about fasting with the major claim that his arrival on earth changes everything – how can they fast while the bridegroom is with them? – and follows this up with two body-blows about the need to cast off their old ways like a worn-out overcoat rather than trying to tack bits of Jesus into their old worldview, and to ensure that they have adequately fresh and flexible wineskins in which to hold the new season's fermentation of Christ's unparalleled vintage.[2] He has then demolished a pharisaic criticism of his followers for plucking grain in the fields on the sabbath (not because it was theft, which it was not, but because rolling the ears in their hands constituted 'threshing' on the sabbath!)

by saying not only that their view was unscriptural and uncharitable, but that the whole debate was now otiose as he could change the rules unilaterally as the sabbath day's maker and lord. He proceeded to heal on the sabbath and in the process challenge the lovelessness with which they used the occasion more to snare Jesus than to reach out help to a sick man.[3] The whole thrust of the section is to confront the conservatism, traditionalism and complacent rationalisation of their culture with the utterly fresh and radical nature of his claims and person. It is in this context that the disciples are called to be apostles[4] and given their ground plan and their marching orders. For the beatitudes and woes uttered by Jesus to be given here (or even to be placed here by Luke's editorial activity) is to give them staggering prominence, and we *have* to make sense of them.

In a nutshell, Luke's beatitudes dangle between Matthew's beatitudes and Luke's woes. Much has been made of the contrast between Matthew's 'poor in spirit' and Luke's 'poor', and although they are probably both valid and closely parallel versions of the Jewish concept and the Aramaic terms, there may well be a shift of emphasis between the two. Whether that is simply editorial, whether the one writer saw a danger of misinterpretation in a political direction and the other feared a Gnostic-style spiritualising of something meant to have more contemporary bite, we cannot know. No preacher would have difficulty in believing that Jesus himself used slightly differing versions of his own sayings or parables in different settings to make slightly different points; it would be odd – and quite at variance with his creativity of mind – if he had not. A slippery lack of clarity in one preacher can be a brilliant highlighting of varied facets in another.

The traditional reading of Matthew's version, beloved of evangelical Christians, goes something like this: The poor in spirit are those who recognise their inner need, the lack in their spirits which can only be made up by God and our dependence on him. They are those who 'know their need of

God'.[5] That line is confirmed by what follows: those who mourn may be those who grieve over the state of the world, but that certainly includes their own sin and leads them to repentance, a mourning for their wrongs before God. Thus they become the meek, people of faith who lean upon God more than on their own strength and insight. They hunger and thirst not for their material gain (whether they started off rich or poor) but for God, for good and for right. Such will be, as they go on, the merciful, the pure in heart, the peacemakers. Certainly those last could be pressed to show a dramatic outworking of the inner changes described, and in the most concrete social settings; but that is most often not done, and even mercy and peacemaking are seen in individualistic categories. As John Stott puts it, 'God may be calling many more Christians than hear his call to immerse themselves in the secular world of politics, economics, sociology, race relations, community health, development and a host of other such spheres for Christ.'[6]

The woes expressed in Luke 6:24–26 seem to live entirely at the other end of the spectrum. Far from focusing on attitudes of heart, they slice into the rich and the well-fed as if those things were themselves causes of judgement. The first of them – 'woe to you who are rich, for you have already received your comfort' – has two echoes in the gospels. There are the Pharisees, 'hypocrites', whose praying the disciples are told in Matthew's sermon not to emulate; for their public display of piety, 'they have received their reward'.[7] Present status or public regard could be bought at the price of deeper things; in seeking the short-term benefit they lost the longer. Likewise the rich man in the parable, when pleading to Abraham for relief, was refused on the grounds that he had had his good things in his earthly life; he too had lost the eternal in the process of obsession with the present. This is just the model Jesus is picking up in his woes, and just the danger against which he is warning. In a way, to have received one's comfort is a tragedy, for that very gift obscures the need to provide for a deeper need by a deeper means. This is not to say that Jesus was against the rich; he did not condemn, despise or avoid the rich, and spent a good deal of time ministering to them and accepting their hospitality. But it is to say that he challenged their bondage to their riches, their possession by their possessions. Riches are in his eyes a massive danger, especially in fostering complacency and callous lack of care for those on whose backs the wealth is made. Truly it was hard for the rich to enter the kingdom; in the same way as some of the camels had to shed their baggage to get through the door at all, some had to shed their dependence on it and their attachment to it, and all had to develop new attitudes not only to their wealth but to those who needed what it could provide.

It is no surprise, therefore, that the second woe also picks up Dives; 'Woe to you who are well fed now, for you will go hungry.' The implication is not that these folk are well-nourished, but that they are grossly and gluttonously fattened by delicacies while unconcerned for others to have their basic needs provided. They have demonstrated that they are not the poor in spirit, for they are not sensitive to the heart of God, nor to the pain of the needy. They are not truly penitent, for to enter the kingdom means to shed selfishness and callous unconcern at the door; they cannot be disciples yet, for the lifestyle of the kingdom has to be one of compassion reaching out to others.

These are those who laugh, not with the healthy mirth of good humour or the joy of celebration, but with the Old Testament's implication of mocking laughter and scorn, contemptuous dismissal of what is right and good or of those who are poor and needy. Those complicit in such betrayal find that all speak well of them, for neither by life nor example nor word are they challenging the status quo around them.

Somewhere between Matthew's beatitudes and Luke's woes we find suspended the Lucan version of the beatitudes.

If Matthew leans to the spiritual, with perhaps a glimpse of social implications, and Luke's woes challenge outrageous social irresponsibility with perhaps a hint of its spiritual roots, Luke has captured in his succinct version of the beatitudes the perfect blend of the two in the mind of Jesus. It was while looking at his disciples that he said, 'Blessed are you who are poor, for yours is the kingdom of God.' The disciples are the key, not because the disciples *are* the poor – that would be far too simple; how anyway could they be the poor if his preaching to the poor were needed to bring them into being? – but they epitomise what it is to be truly poor in the Bible's eyes. That Old Testament combination of submissive attitude before God and likely practical deprivation is theirs in the neatest form. They hold the kingdom of God only because they have met its terms of entry; because they have submitted to the king. The spiritual side of that is to have forsaken spiritual self-sufficiency, recognised their need of God and come through repentance to trust him. They are the poor in spirit. But the practical side of that is that in hearing the call to repentance they had borne its fruit, forsaking greed and the pursuit of material wealth in the process of following Jesus. The disciples included, after all, not only Levi who had left exploitation and intimidation of the poor to follow Jesus, but also an assortment of middle-class Galilean boat-owners and entrepreneurs whose discipleship cost them a long-planned lifestyle. So 'you who hunger now' is also two-edged; as disciples, by definition they hungered for righteousness – but they had also lost a lifestyle of ease and security. 'You who weep' is likewise a blanket term for all those who need or see the need for God's intervention in history – those who weep over their own sin and corruption as well as those who grieve for the pain of the world, its deprivation and oppression, and who find joy in seeing God at work in whatever dimension of human liberation.

These of course are those who find men hating them. As

those of whom all men speak well are those who present no challenge to the values and assumptions of their culture, those who lay that challenge find the very resistance which was offered to Jesus: 'If the world hates me, it will hate you also'.[8] The poor in spirit are unpopular if they renounce pride and achievement and live for Jesus and his values of love and service; all the more so if in the process they challenge materialism and its attendant corruption and exploitation.

It is on this basis that Jesus can lay down some of his most specific and searching discipleship teaching. A generous heart towards opponents, mercy to those in need, an uncondemning mind, forgiveness of others' hurts upon one, generous giving in every setting; these are the fruits which appropriately grow on a tree rooted in such depth of self-abandonment to the will, the love and the knowledge of God.[9] To practise these things is to build with a solidity all too rare in the long history of Christian superficiality.[10]

Such a basis for the disciple's life is reiterated throughout the gospel. It involves the pain and publicity of bearing the sign of Jesus' death,[11] freedom from the binding ties of property, custom and family,[12] availability to a travelling-light, commando-style ministry under the Lord's immediate summons,[13] a deep reliance on God and his resources[14] to the point where the disciple has power to confront every sign of darkness and dispel it with love and light.[15] It involves knowing chalk from cheese,[16] a life of integrity[17] and courage in God in the face of whatever comes,[18] moving in the power of God's own Spirit;[19] it involves freedom from anxiety and fear,[20] resolute priorities,[21] material sacrifice and love for the needy.[22] It involves discipline and alertness, ready for the work of service, the pain of division, the stresses of the times and the return of Christ alike.[23] Generosity,[24] purity,[25] faith[26] and faithfulness,[27] humility[28] and a constant eye to what God is doing;[29] these, capped always by a sense of fellowship with Christ[30] and involvement in his mission to the world,[31] characterise the disciple.

The parables and the power

Those vivid cameos of truth, the parables, I have kept aside
from the thrust of the sermon on the plain and its follow-on to
have a look at them by themselves. We have touched on a
number of them in chapter four, but there is a worth in
surveying their main points in isolation to see exactly what
Jesus used them for. It is commonly said by the scholars that
a parable only teaches one vivid point; as a safeguard against
rampant allegory that is fair comment. As we have noticed,
though, Jesus often used them to teach at more than one
level at once, and we should not be mentally boxed by an
unqualified assertion. However, because the main thrust of
each is clear enough there is value in clumping them together
according to the main thing they are each trying to do.

The generosity of God. While Luke does not give us the supreme
New Testament parable of grace, that of the labourers in the
vineyard,[32] he has the same truth powerfully in the shepherd,
the woman after her coin and the lost son's father;[33] and by
contrast with the reluctant friend in bed,[34] the unjust
judge,[35] and the unlikely moneylender.[36] Several of these,
especially in Luke 15, are used in defence of Jesus' ministry
among the outcast, basing his action on the character of a
God who specialises in those kinds of poor.

The growth of the kingdom. The very fact that God chooses such
unlikely material may explain the apparently hidden growth
of Jesus' movement, for many of his critics would find it
beneath them to observe God's work in the kinds of clients
Jesus had. But there is also an intrinsically hidden character
to the kingdom for its roots, if not its fruit, are hidden in the
soil of the human heart. Hence the sower[37] and the other
agricultural metaphors, the mustard seed and its parallel
message of the yeast in the lump.[38]

The response to Jesus. If the kingdom grows like that, each individual's response to the challenge to enter it is of paramount importance: he must build on the rock,[39] bear unhindered grain,[40] pass through the door,[41] accept the divine invitation,[42] weigh up the cost of building or battling for Christ,[43] come to himself and go home to God,[44] beat his breast and find forgiveness.[45] But the response is not initial only; there is a call to faithful persistence too. The tree must bear its right fruit year by year,[46] the word must be practised,[47] the lamp shine,[48] the house of life be fully occupied by the new management.[49] The servant must be active and faithful.[50] Such faithfulness is contrasted with the negative attitude and conduct of those who will not make room for Jesus, who build on sand,[51] are confident in their own righteousness,[52] cache their assets,[53] or – most bluntly of all – hijack what God has entrusted to them and do not understand that they will be called to account.[54]

Riches a danger. Among the many things which may hold back a person from a suitable response to God's intervention in the world in the kingdom of Christ, riches are high on the list. Maybe their superficiality deters a man from digging deep enough when he builds his dwelling;[55] certainly they throttle growth,[56] distort perspectives and foster folly,[57] distract from the banquet,[58] lead into dissipation,[59] desensitise compassion and condemn to hell.[60]

Care for the poor. Nowhere more than in Luke are the parables used to teach bluntly the social implications of discipleship. When the response is made, the restraints of bondage to sin or materialism loosed, and obedience begins, it has specific and wide-ranging implications. Not only does Jesus justify his own ministry among the outcast, he sends his followers there by vivid command. They are not to despise the outcast,[61] but to scrape them off the roadside[62] even – or especially – when their race, language, history or social standing is alien. The lost and the alienated are precise targets of ministry.[63] The rich man in his castle has no business to leave the poor man at his gate;[64] he should have had him to dinner.[65]

No fudging the issue. Although Luke does not spend as much time warning about the final judgement as his co-evangelists Matthew or even Mark, nor does he pass on the harrowing parable of the sheep and the goats,[66] there is no question of suggesting that either neglect, personal sin or injustice will be overlooked in the last analysis. It will be good for servants whose master finds them watching and serving when he comes.[67] A jerry-built life collapses,[68] an unfruitful tree is cut down,[69] the banquet is closed[70] and the door sealed.[71] Dives burns,[72] the idle are stripped[73] and unworthy tenants lose their lives.[74]

In sum, the parables teach what Jesus always teaches: that God is breaking in in his Son, that his coming is drastically new, and that response to him is crucial. The response has to be deeply Godward and therefore of the Spirit; but it impinges on every part of a man's life and relationship, claiming to correct them all, to replace the old coat with a new. And that will be so thoroughgoing that it will transform all his attitudes, and with them his landholding and investments, his eating and drinking, his vision and action towards every neighbour he has. The inwardness of his life will be turned inside out towards the poor.

6 PRIORITIES TRANSMITTED

Emerging from Emmanuel Presbyterian after a particularly moving multiracial and multilingual service, at which a fiery exposition of the woes on the powerful had accompanied a jubilant welcome to a recently released long-stay Robben Island prisoner, Zipho flung down his gauntlet, 'What's the point of talking on about what Jesus said, when his followers are so unlike him? Most of the churches in this city are a thousand miles from obeying his words. They are just a social phenomenon thrown up by our religious needs and hooked on to Jesus' name by their cultural history – they don't want to take him seriously at all.'

Driving past St Agnes', it was awkward for Simon to respond to that. The people coming out were all white, if only because most of them kept their domestics working until after Sunday lunch had been served and cleared. They weren't walking home, and only a few more were driving cheap or ancient cars. The impact of their worship on their lifestyle looked embarrassingly small, and on society's values even less. As they turned the corner by Corybantic Chapel, the picture was almost identical, but for some younger faces and more informal clothing. The so-called renewal of the church in which Pentecostals and charismatics have become involved seemed to be pretty selective in what it wanted to renew.

Was Jesus, then, entirely divorced from the church which bore his name? And if so, was that because he never intended it to follow the thrust of his own work, or because it was having trouble in itself in discerning and obeying his will?

141

These two issues – the intention of Christ for his church and the current ferment in its thinking – form the themes of this and the following chapter.

In what form did Jesus bequeath his priorities to his followers? It is curious that for all their rootedness in the life and teaching of Jesus, almost all the strands of Christian tradition have presupposed in practice a qualitative chasm between the life of Jesus and the era of the church. Those with a Catholic outlook, for all their emphasis on the incarnation, are curiously far from the programme of Jesus' earthly life. Those with a Protestant/evangelical theology draw a decisive line between what Jesus did and how his people witness to it. Charismatics and Pentecostals (forgetting the insights of Edward Irving) focus so much on the coming of the Spirit at Pentecost that his previous activities are lost from view, and despite their doctrinal demolition of dispensationalism they invent their own species of it in effect. The liberationists do it the other way round; although they can be nearer at times to the directness and relevance of the teaching and work in which Jesus engaged than some of their more 'religious' contemporaries, they can be so wrapped up in letting the world write the church's agenda that they battle to make sense of large tracts of what Jesus was about. In each case there is a theological hiatus somewhere between the hills of Galilee and the post-Pentecost church which, for all that it expresses a certain truth, neglects the continuities.

In many ways, of course, the New Testament itself can give an impression of discontinuity. Matthew and Mark, however much they may have embodied the concerns of the later church, stop their stories dead at the ascension of Jesus; Paul, although scholars may have exaggerated his neglect of the earthly Jesus in favour of the cosmic Christ, does have his focus on both the spiritual and the terrestrial situation which obtained for the Christians of his day and leans little on the evidence of the incarnate life of Jesus before Calvary in his writing. It is left to Luke and John in different and largely neglected ways to stress some of the continuity.

Take John first, as a context in which to speak of Luke. One way of viewing the so-called farewell discourses and high-priestly prayer in John 13–17 is to see them precisely as Jesus' own manifesto for the future continuation of the very things he has been about in his earthly ministry. As he washes his disciples' feet, they are to learn that once washed in his ministry they will only need to dip their extremities in order to remain in the cleansed relationship which he has inaugurated. Out of that they are to go on ministering to each other in exactly his way. If that prevails, men will know that the disciples go on belonging to him, even when he appears to have departed. It is just his impending departure which causes Jesus the pastoral concern to reassure the disciples that all will still be well; he is only going a little ahead, will return to take them on with him and in the meanwhile will send a replacement reinforcement (a fairly exact translation of John 14:16's 'another Counsellor') to enable them to go on doing the works he has done and to expand them. The mission will clearly neither stop dead nor change dramatically. The interwoven relationship of Father, Son, Spirit and people will not dissolve, but if anything intensify, to the point where the life and sap of a plant – such as a vine – is now a more accurate image than that of a shepherd with individual sheep. They must go on remaining in him and in his word, the very word which the coming substitute for Jesus – the Spirit – will lead them in. Their love, their mission, their activities and their persecution are but extensions of his. His words on the Spirit so permeate these chapters that his promise to come to them is likely to be meant of Pentecost at least as much as of the resurrection (and more than of the second coming). Thus in the prayer in John 17, his followers have so much crossed a line from the world's side to Christ's that they need protection in continuing in a role of presence and witness in the world which parallels, or rather extends, the very things Jesus has done himself; they will face the same temptations, the same opposition, and the same opportunities precisely because they are and will continue to be, in a deep and multifaceted sense, *his*. His whole plan was that they might reach the place where he is *in them*, just as he has promised that his Spirit will be in or among them. The unity and continuity of master and servants, indweller and indwelt, stock and branches, could not be more eloquently put.

It is just this sense of essential continuity between Jesus and his followers, and thus between his work and theirs, which Luke is concerned to communicate. Not only does he overlap his gospel and his second volume, the Acts, so that the ascension and the last commission to his work act as the hinge between the panels of the diptych, but he shapes the Acts account (not woodenly but with brilliant artistry) to pick up the pattern of the first volume.

At the outset of Acts, in case we should miss the point, Luke sums up his gospel as 'all that Jesus *began* to do and to teach'.[1] The inference is clear that what follows is not the acts of the apostles, but what Jesus *continued* to do and to teach. He then proceeds to show us that Jesus gave the apostles the very same commission that he had accepted for himself. Just as the Spirit of the Lord was upon him to anoint him, so they would 'receive power when the Holy Spirit comes';[2] if he needed that, how much more did they? As the purpose of his anointing was that he might proclaim good news, so theirs would equip them to 'be my witnesses'. Both phrases may appear at first to speak of a verbal ministry only; but we have seen that for Jesus to proclaim was both to speak and to bring into being the effect of his speaking – healing for Mary, sight for Bartimaeus, justice for Jericho, food for Lazarus, salvation for all of them and a new community of faith and love in the bargain. The apostles, significantly, were not *to witness* but to *be witnesses* (*esesthe mou martures*); that includes what Peter later called giving a reasoned defence (*apologia*) for their hope,[3] but it was wider. They were to *be* first, and their being would speak as much as their doing or saying. It was not as if their private lives were divorced from their preaching, as Pharisees from that day to this have tried to compartmentalise things; their whole existence was to bear testimony to Jesus, and their testimony was to bring into being not hearers only but whole-life witnesses in turn. Nothing less was the gospel.

As for the range of their target area, it also corresponds to his. We have seen that when he set off to proclaim good news to the poor, he had in mind both a specific category within Israel and a wide band of human need which puts the broadest construction on such terms as the blind, the prisoners and the oppressed. As we have seen, this is not to spiritualise those terms but to affirm that they may be neither spiritualised nor politicised as the terminology is too broad to be drained of either their material or their spiritual content – or, for that matter, any other content across the spectrum in between. In Acts the same truth is expressed in geographical terms; they are to be his witnesses in Jerusalem, Judea, Samaria and to the ends of the earth. No doubt those terms had a symbolic significance, Jerusalem for the immediate locality and their place of recent failure, Judea perhaps for the desert or the rural areas, Samaria for the despised community where they could not begin to expect acceptance. But they were also geographical circles – rippling out until everyone on earth had received the witness of Jesus and had made their own response. It is quite gratuitous to limit that response to the straightforward 'religious' response of a Peter leaving home to follow Jesus; it has to incorporate the worldwide Levis who must change their occupation, the Zacchaeuses who must rectify social evil, the Diveses who must change their lifestyle and priorities, as well as the Bartimaeuses who find new vision and follow it with joy down the road. I have some sympathy with the white South African medical missionary friend in Lesotho who wishes we had kept the KJV's translation, 'unto the uttermost part of the earth', for it somehow captures the all-exploring and all-inclusive expectation of Christ that his followers would fulfil. It is not too much to say, when we grasp what the poor meant in Jesus' mind and ministry, that his 'ends of the earth' here are just the same group of people – the needy of the earth in all their multiform hurts and lostness.

Such a ministry is exactly what the apostles proceed to exercise. It is nowhere clearer than on the day of Pentecost, though later instances confirm and extend the picture. As at Jesus' baptism, the day begins with an existential trans-formation through spiritual experience. Just as he had promised, the power comes and anoints the disciples who (for once) have done as they were told and waited (in both senses) for just that. They proceed to proclaim good news to the poor in the person of Peter, who becomes, as promised, a witness in Jerusalem.[4] His hearers, responding, must do just what John's and Jesus' hearers had to do for release from the oppression of sin. More than in John's and Jesus' work, they are then explicitly and immediately able to embrace the gift of God now poured out in the Spirit, with all his benefits. And the effect? After baptism they proceed to a quite unforeseen (by them) lifestyle in which they learn from the apostles (there is still a verbal ministry to the poor unenlightened), they are involved in a sharing of life so weakly rendered by the English word 'fellowship', they break the bread of common meals and of the Messiah with each other, and learn to know God in prayer. With that come wonders and signs through which the poor sick and the poor bound are set free, and the generosity of the new community not only brings in a new form of jubilee unbidden but outstrips the demands of Mosaic justice in a tidal wave of love. No Lazaruses lie on the doorsteps of these people, no Levis hold their corruptly gotten gains, no lame or blind or crippled or poor remain uninvited to the banquet. It is no wonder that they enjoyed the people's favour, nor that the Lord added to their number.

Jubilee has come and the poor have good news preached to them; the signs of the kingdom are there because the king is enthroned and his law obeyed from a glad heart. Yet the cost of all that to the rich and landed, the cost in cash and reversed assumptions and peer-group unpopularity and radical new relationship, should not be missed. The fruits of repentance were real, sore and revolutionary, and without them there was no repentance worth the name and no forgiveness in baptism, for it was a baptism into a new community, a new lifestyle and a new obedience as well as into the 'religious' dimension of Jesus Christ.

Nowhere else in Acts is the picture so neat or striking, and of course Christians have made up varying accounts of the decline from that early shared lifestyle ranging from 'getting back to sanity' across to idealising it as the day to which Christians should long since have returned. The rest of Acts is more concerned to describe the stages of growth in both extent and perceptions in the early church than to highlight the balance of its ministry, yet the breadth of that ministry is all the more telling in cropping up incidentally.

In the Jerusalem church, for example, the poor sick appear early on[5] being healed, and quite explicitly as a continuation of the personal work of Jesus.[6] With it there is preaching,[7] a challenge to the abuse of power,[8] miraculous power[9] and care for the hungry, bereaved and elderly.[10] All this is part of the ministry they have inherited from Jesus, a role of which they are perfectly conscious: 'We are witnesses of these things, and so is the Holy Spirit, whom God has given to those who obey him', Acts 5:32. Indeed the previous verse, Acts 5:31, is a deliberate echo of their commission as given in Luke 24:46–49.

The concentric circles then begin to develop as planned and commanded. The poor Samaritans are reached, preached to and brought to receive the same Spirit the apostles had.[11] Saul is won, healed, taught, *and reconciled*: the poor rich persecutor becomes the rich poor persecuted.[12] Woes turn to beatitudes. Disciples continue to help the poor.[13] And eventually the poor Gentiles, whom Jesus has spoken of in the Nazareth synagogue to the accompaniment of much indignation and to whom he had himself begun to minister, are decisively incorporated into the Spirit and the church through Peter 'telling the good news of peace through Jesus Christ'.[14] As he says, Jesus 'commanded us to preach to the people', and it was only in doing so that they found out fully who the people were whom Jesus wanted to reach – no longer an ethnic group but 'everyone who believes in him' may come in.[15]

That same ministry seems to have sprung up spon-taneously at Antioch,[16] where preaching and teaching are soon complemented by the very practical generosity that was seen at the beginning, this time for the poor Jewish hungry.[17] This ties up with the recurring theme in Paul's letters about the collection for the poor in Jerusalem which is often relegated in the church's exegesis to dedicated Sunday giving, and yet is in fact a symptom of the nature of the early church and the breadth of its ministry. The poor are never incidental but constitutive. They could always say with Paul, 'they asked . . . that we should continue to remember the poor, the very thing I was eager to do'.[18]

One could elaborate from the Acts – on the attention paid to women, the challenge given to the rich and greedy ('You fool' was never spoken so firmly as to Ananias and Sapphira), the oblique rebuke to the abuse of power in the whole saga of Paul's arrest and trials, the commitment to each other in the ministry presupposed by the relation-ships in the missionary band and between them and their support-base churches, and more. Enough stands, when reinforced by the epistles of John and Paul, to sustain the claim that the ministry of the church was in its aims and recipients an exact follow-on from the ministry and priorities of Jesus himself. And that is because their commission was just the same; the vision of Isaiah became the mantle of

Jesus, and he in turn lifted it from Nazareth to the mount of ascension to place it on the shoulders of his church. It remains to be asked what the church has done with it and, if it has mislaid it at least in part, what can be done to rediscover and reapply it.

7   AGENDA DEBATED

If the call of the Christian church is anything like what these chapters have suggested, there are a thousand reasons why Christians should have had trouble over the years in keeping to it.

For a start, despite the simple version, it is not so easy to grasp theologically. The very variety of the splendid insights and exhortations in the scriptures inclines us to seize on some which strike us and lead us to miss the whole: it is, after all, the greatest conceptual system for understanding reality, and the finest vision of how human life may be lived, that the world has yet encountered. Besides that, each Christian has his personal background, of which he is understandably jealous and by which he has inevitably been formed; the subcultural teachings and assumptions he has learnt are not easily shed for a bigger picture.

I owe the basis of my own Christian learning to evangelical circles, and my very love and debt towards them makes it hard, I know, to outgrow some of what I know to be prejudice. For the best reasons my mentors believed that social benefits were *by-products* of the gospel – good, necessary, valuable, even required by God – but by-products all the same. I no longer believe that, simply on the good evangelical ground that it is not a biblical view; for me the social implications are of the *essence* of the faith, and I cannot un-believe that without re-writing the great commandment on which hang all the law and the prophets so dearly loved of my teachers. The corporate social aspect is a constitutive part of God's plan of salvation. Yet for me that shift of perceptions was slow and costly. How much slower it could therefore be for someone with less opportunity for exposure to theological reading and debate, or for someone with a forcefully limiting intellectual peer group (such as a sect or narrow-visioned church), or for someone with far greater material vested interests than I will ever have, is hard to overestimate.

It is thus not hard to see how the assumptions of the landed classes in Europe throughout the middle ages (for example) have deeply coloured every European's expectations about the shape that Christian responsibility should take. The condition of the pre-revolutionary church in Russia, the need for a confessing church in Hitler's Germany, the awkward position of the Roman Catholics in South America today, the sparks that fly in our synods in the South African churches – all are so readily understandable. Our minds no less than our structures have capitulated to the worldliness of the day; and they may surrender to today's socialism as much as to yesterday's capitalism, colonialism or feudalism.

There have of course been many attempts to unscramble our thinking and recover the church's identity and vision. This chapter is given to reviewing a number of schools of thought in today's church.

The view from Recife

Undoubtedly the greatest intellectual shake-up the Christian church has faced about its agenda in recent years has come from South America, in the phenomenon known broadly as liberation theology. In a nutshell the origins of liberation theology lay in the difficulty which South American Christians were having in seeing the relevance of the gospel in their life setting. It seemed that the good news was not only rooted in the Bible but framed in the culture and conditions of western Europe, and appeared to address a bad news remote from the day-to-day bad news of the people's experience of life around them. Certainly the alienation between man and God of which that gospel spoke might need to be addressed, but somehow the links between that and the other more pressing alienations of daily life – between landowner and peasant, employer and worker, man and woman, army and civilian, the labourer and the fruit of his work – needed to make sense too. Some saw that this was a problem of what is called hermeneutics – that is, of how we enable the content of the scriptures and the place where we live to address each other in a way that brings meaning, truth and guidance from the one to the other. For years Catholics and Protestants had been arguing about whether the Bible's meaning could be understood from its pages through the interpretation of the church to the people, or directly by the people being exposed to the Bible for themselves. But they both began with the Bible, or at least with the self-disclosure of God on earth of which it speaks. Some in South America began to insist that the formulations of both these essentially western approaches overlooked a factor in the equation, namely the life-situation of the hearer, which was often throwing up questions which the teachers' answers were not addressing. They wanted to come to the Bible, questions in hand, looking for answers or guidance which would speak to their situation head-on. Thus some of South America's theologians began to speak of a 'hermeneutical circle'; the former concept of a straight line from Bible to life was to be replaced by more of a mutual approach in which, at best, the pain of men's lives could come to the scriptures and question, just as the scriptures themselves might initiate input (through the reader, the preacher, or some synod of the church) into the place where the people were sitting.

The early stages of liberation theology were pioneered by Roman Catholic thinkers, joined quickly by various evangelicals and later others. Back in the 1960s the Roman Catholic Archbishop of Recife in Brazil, Dom Helder Camara, drew the attention of both media and disquieted secular authorities when he began to spell out some of the church's need to align itself with the poor and underprivileged. He gave many an intellectual key to thinking about violence in days when it was easy for oppressive regimes to discourage resistance by branding opponents as initiators of violence. Archbishop Camara pointed out that in many states a rebel's turning to arms was but a response to the methods of his oppressor, what he christened 'Violence Two', in a situation where 'Violence One' was not only the responsibility but the favoured methodology of the regime. In this way armed revolt might on occasion be an aspect of the just war which much of Christian history has supported.

The name of Gustavo Gutierrez, a theologian in Peru, was also breaking on the theological scene in the early 1970s; he has proved one of the most articulate and thoughtful of liberation theology's spokesmen. He defines liberation theology as thinking 'based on the Gospel and the experiences of men and women committed to the process of liberation in the oppressed and exploited land of Latin America; it is a theological reflection born . . . of shared efforts to abolish the current unjust situation and to build a different society, freer and more human'.[1] This vital interplay between the agony of the situation and the deposit of the scriptures has been worked over with greater or less clarity both by Roman Catholic thinkers such as Hugo Assmann, J. L. Segundo and J. P. Miranda, and by significant evangelical figures like Orlando Costas and José Miguez-Bonino. They all challenge the western theology imported into their world as theoretical, boxed into the pastoral rather than the prophetic, inclined to the status quo, and individualistic. As a result they are inclined to maximise the societal dimensions of biblical salvation language, to see sin in its corporate as much as its personal aspects, and to view Marxist perceptions of society with favour.

This last has, of course, given the whole movement a

convenient bad name in many quarters; however it is few of these thinkers who would embrace a Marxist-socialist programme necessarily as the best *solution* to their problems. They are simply saying that Marx's analysis of the causes of human grief worldwide has been of exceptional value in the last century, and that its adherents have all too often been moved by greater compassion to more effective action than the followers of the carpenter of Nazareth. That, they say, is neither his fault nor the Bible's; it lies in the extent to which so-called Christians have been so wedded to the thinking and assumptions of the colonial capitalist west, that their capacity to respond with his compassion has been compromised to vanishing point. In their attempts to release the Bible from its imprisonment in the thought-forms of that culture they have turned to the themes of Exodus, the social teaching of Amos and Isaiah, the ministry of Jesus and some of his less-read teaching, and the often-buried implications of the New Testament's understanding of man, salvation, the church and the kingdom. Sometimes their exegesis has been over-enthusiastic to the point of distortion, and as subjective as that of those they criticise;[2] often it has been all too perceptive and thought-provoking.

They have, for example, challenged the spiritualising understanding of Paul's teaching on principalities and powers, which have traditionally been understood as supernatural demonic forces of evil opposed to the purposes of God. Liberation theologians have questioned whether in fact he could have been referring instead to such social phenomena as economic forces, public opinion, military violence, government or multinational corporations. The debate continues and the theological consensus is certainly not persuaded to accept their thesis wholesale; yet there is a far greater readiness to believe at least that the supernatural forces may play upon the others to malicious purpose, or at most that there is some kind of continuum between the two.

The whole world of liberation theology is sufficiently new and varied that no one can say it has been definitively accepted or rejected by global Christian thinking. Rather, parts of its emphasis and various of its proponents' ideas have been found convincing and challenging by the wider Christian mind in today's world, and much of its approach has been taken very seriously in widely varied church and political situations. One of their most telling interpretations has been of Jesus' theme in John 3:21 and 7:17, 'whoever lives by the truth comes into the light . . . If anyone chooses to do God's will, he will find out whether my teaching comes from God'. The stress that knowing is not separate from living and doing but depends on it has led to the coming of the term 'orthopraxis' – right action – alongside the old term 'orthodoxy', right belief. The Latin Americans have been telling the church that unless one is committed to discipleship he cannot be said to be functioning Christianly. The novel thrust in this is that they point out that, spiritual dimensions apart, the basic framework of the life of any twentieth-century man is politically and economically determined. That being so, true discipleship has to be that which is committed to the will of God for society; and in many countries of the world, that has to mean a solid commitment to social change as the basis of Christian conduct. Theology – God-talk – may only be attempted from that posture. That challenge will stand as the hermeneutical and political debates continue.

The view from Rome

Until quite recently the Roman Catholic Church could have been characterised as one of the world's most socially conformist and politically conservative institutions; it was implicated, for example, in the support of many of the grim Latin American regimes which its own theologians on the spot came to find themselves condemning. It has been the frontline involvement of many Catholics, and not least numerous priests, in the local affairs of many a downtrodden community which has linked up with a major theological re-think at headquarters to turn the Catholic Church into what many regimes have come rightly to regard as a highly subversive body. Criticism of both the old and the new theology will continue, not least from Protestant/evangelical quarters, and some of the motives for the Catholic Church's trendy stances will also be called in question, but there is no doubt that the Roman Catholic Church has found a prophetic profile and a commitment to the underprivileged in recent years which has set it at the forefront of both social theology and local political action in many countries.

The South American scene which we have touched on, Pope John Paul II's links behind the Iron Curtain, and the way in which the Catholic Bishops' Conference in South Africa has in many ways caught the torch of social courage as it fell from Anglican hands, are all symptomatic of a vast change of line. Where the social encyclicals from the Vatican would once automatically affirm the right of private property and step cautiously round any suggestion that it could be abused, such recent pieces as *Redemptor Hominis* are ready to explore what salvation means for man in all the dimensions of his life, including the challenge of that to socio-economic and political oppression anywhere. No doubt there are some conservative local manifestations and some hard debates behind closed doors; but for an outfit of that size the Catholics have made a sea-turn of remarkable dimensions in a short time, and the next few years will be intriguing.

The view from Liverpool

In Britain one of Catholicism's most visible leaders has been Archbishop Derek Worlock of Liverpool, whose close association with Anglican Bishop David Sheppard has been exemplary. Bishop Sheppard has given us, in his *Built as a City* and more recently in his liberationist-sounding *Bias to the Poor*, an urban-Western perspective which fits into the cry of the poor from the Third World.[3] It is not only where a bloated oligarchy suppresses the vast rural peasantry that God cares for the downtrodden; there have been many manifestations in the stale and jaded world of the industrial or post-industrial West.

In *Bias to the Poor*, Bishop Sheppard tries to link the theological conviction that God has a special burden for the materially poor to this urban-Western need. Out of his own experience in inner-city London and Liverpool he highlights some of the real deprivation of opportunity, hope, creativity and conditions as well as material goods which goes on among the aged, unemployed or racial minorities in the cities of the West. He points out that the conventional perception of society as a pyramid with the poor as the broadest section at the base is erroneous; these days western societies, and certainly Britain, are more like a diamond with a reasonably well-off broad band of unionised workers in the middle. The poor are fewer than they were but even more disadvantaged, for the unions which used to champion justice and the interests of their members when those two things were more often than not identical, now stick to championing their interests with often unjust effects. They are generally not there to champion the real underdog, who slips into despair and apathy – which Bishop Sheppard neatly defines as 'a kind of frozen violence'.[4]

As with Third World protests, the great boon of Bishop Sheppard's book is his own exposure to the real pain of people for whom he feels. The somewhat anecdotal nature of the book (and, be it said, of his theological case) does not detract from the sharpness of his critique of the effects of liberal capitalism which claims to benefit all but rarely does so. He is also careful to offer a critique of Marxism but gives a useful summary of its common ground with Christianity, the very things which have drawn the two so close in Latin America:

> The belief that man is a social being, with longings that his gifts should be used for the community and recognised by the community.
> The realisation that the economic and social structures of society can form the minds and shape the destinies of those who are subject to them.
> The questioning of who controls the means of production, and to whom they are accountable.
> An indignation at unequal distribution of wealth and opportunity.
> A belief in a better future order.
> A longing for a realistic programme, which the poor especially can strive after.[5]

Aware that Latin America's theologians are open to the criticism of using the Bible with cavalier regard to its own meaning and values, he offers his own hermeneutical circle:

> This is described as a circle because its different parts should keep on relating to each other. Here are four parts of a circle of interpretation:
> 1. Pay attention to the world of ideas and experience of the Biblical writer and his readers. What glasses did they wear?
> 2. Notice the ways in which people today, including ourselves, are conditioned by our experience of life and of the particular Church tradition to which we belong. What glasses do we wear?
> 3. Commit ourselves to action in obedience to what we believe God is saying to our particular situation; and reflect critically on our action and the theory from

which it stems. This is what Liberation Theology writers call *praxis*.
4. Let the Biblical text speak back to the questions we bring to it.[6]

In particular Bishop Sheppard calls the Christian church to pay heed to the racial issue which is less to the forefront in South America but very much with the church in North America and Europe, as well as in its tribal manifestations throughout Africa – apart from the cauldron of the South. The place of Jews and Gentiles in a multiracial church has a significance deeper than is usually recognised. It is here that Bishop Sheppard helpfully picks up the issue of social solidarity, which impinges in different contexts on Black Consciousness. Maybe weakened groups need to be brought together in community in order to find their identity through shared experience, but if those groupings leave out the global nature of the church of Jesus Christ in all its multicoloured glory, they may reinforce perceptions which undermine the work of God. That way lie ethnic churches and apartheid.

Perhaps because he has been seen in England as forsaking his own evangelical background, Bishop Sheppard confronts the question of whether the gospel is essentially about changing individuals or transforming structures and concludes that it is both. 'For the Church to hear the cry of the poor will mean losing its innocence on social and political matters,' but 'Christianity is both about justice and about Christ changing people from inside out.'[7] The church which the world needs is one which:

Stays present in the neediest areas and continues to believe and worship.
Recognises, develops and supports local ability within the Church and outside it.
Serves people where they are.

Tries to understand, and obey the word of God for both rich and poor.[8]

The vision is good, the heart warm, and the experience long enough that we are given not only the cry but some tried suggestions for ministering to the situation. No one could fail to be sympathetic with the concept of relative poverty which Bishop Sheppard expounds, when most of society is strong and the bottom of the pile is an uncomfortable place to be, especially when the materialism of society dangles perpetually unattainable goods before the poor man's eyes on every hoarding and TV programme. Still, the view from outside the industrial west (and north) has some difficulty; a relocated black South African with neither money nor roof, clothing nor medicine, food nor water, might look askance at a Liverpudlian flat-dweller having trouble extracting her full social security benefits from the local bureaucracy. Still, as we have seen, Jesus knew that human distress comes in many forms, and was interested in it all.

The view from Melbourne

The World Council of Churches found its beginnings in the Edinburgh Missionary Conference in 1910. One of its major sections, the Commission on World Mission and Evangelism, held its March conference in Melbourne in May 1980. The meeting needs to be compared with another in the following month, but for now we should notice that many would regard this conference as the high-water mark of social-liberationist perceptions of the church's mission and agenda in the life of the WCC. That judgement is, of course, an over-simplification; there are too many Christians with too many theological perspectives involved in the World Council for any monochrome view to dominate. Still, the emphases of liberation theology have taken firm hold in CWME in recent years. The topics for the four sections of the Melbourne conference make the point:

1. Good News to the Poor
2. The Kingdom of God and Human Struggles
3. The Church witnesses to the Kingdom
4. The Crucified Christ challenges Human Power

One wonders what most of the delegates to the Edinburgh Missionary Conference would have made of those! Further, the debate focussed largely around human rights and socio-economic issues, with many delegates from western countries bemoaning the poor record of their nations in doing anything about the predicament of the bulk of the world's population or taking to heart (for example) the report of the Brandt Commission. For those who see the whole debate about the church's agenda in terms of 'ecumenicals versus evangelicals', this epitomised the former and alarmed the latter, who found little enough about personal faith and salvation, an unfamiliar meaning to the term 'evangelism', and disturbing politicising and secularising in the whole affair. There were, as is often said about the WCC, all too few evangelical Christians there to make these points and more positive ones of their own; but the criticism came not only from them. For example the emphasis on the dignity of the poor led to a warning from Japanese theologian Kosume Koyama:

When the poor are elevated to the height of history, when all humanity is centred by the presence of the poor, when the poor are the only mediators through whom we are to come to God in Christ, a new idolatry has been created of which the poor themselves are unaware. Then humanity is divided into two faceless sections: the rich and the poor.[9]

So can the recovery of a much-needed balance overturn into untruth.

The theme of the conference had been the prayer, 'Your Kingdom Come!' It was left to Metropolitan Anthony of the Orthodox Church to comment, 'everything that could remotely be related to this theme – political, economic, social – was considered, but the Gospel concept of the Kingdom of God was considered least of all'.[10]

The view from Lausanne

Just a month after Melbourne there took place in Pattaya in Thailand a Consultation on World Evangelization, the second major gathering organised by the Lausanne Committee for World Evangelization whose first meeting had been (of course) in Lausanne, in 1974. This is clearly one of the major joint projects of the world's evangelical Christians in our day, seeking to do what they perceive the ecumenical constituency are leaving undone – the proclamation of a gospel of salvation to a world whose individuals need to hear and respond to it in personal faith.

It is perhaps unfair to compare Melbourne and Pattaya, for the latter was not so much theological as methodological; Lausanne had laid the plan, now its implementation was in view. Consequently its theme was method – 'How shall they hear?' – and its work was divided up according to groups around the world who were deemed to need to be 'reached' with the Christian message, including Hindus, Marxists, mystics, city-dwellers, and thirteen other such groups. Nevertheless comparison invites itself and can be done; it is most illuminating in the area of theological presuppositions, that is, the assumptions about God, man, the world and the gospel which were being made. One of only twenty or so Christians who attended both conferences was Professor David Bosch of South Africa and his comparison has become something of a classic in mission studies.[11]

In a nutshell, Professor Bosch sums up Melbourne as having focused on man's present needs, social change, corporate sin, liberation, action, the poor, seeing Jesus in his earthly life and his parallels with man's present situation, and tending to socialism politically; whereas he saw Pattaya as emphasising man's spiritual needs, religious life, personal sin, salvation, preaching, the lost, seeing Jesus through the eyes of Paul as the once and future saviour now apart from man in glory, and tending politically to capitalism. Melbourne saw humanisation as mission and almost lost sight of evangelism; Pattaya saw mission as evangelism with social involvement as either a partner, a preparation or a consequence of it. Of course, Pattaya embraced a spectrum of viewpoints, though perhaps less wide than Melbourne; but Professor Bosch detected a backtracking even from Lausanne, where a strong commitment to social action was incorporated in the Lausanne Covenant:

> We affirm that God is both the Creator and the Judge of all men. We therefore should share his concern for justice and reconciliation throughout human society and for the liberation of men from every kind of oppression . . . Although reconciliation with man is not reconciliation with God, nor is social action evangelism, nor is political liberation salvation, nevertheless we affirm that evangelism and socio-political involvement are both part of our Christian duty. For both are necessary expressions of our doctrines of God and man, our love for our neighbour and our obedience to Jesus Christ . . . The salvation we claim should be transforming us in the totality of our personal and social responsibilities. Faith without words is dead.[12]

For all the unity behind the Covenant, it seems that different groups of evangelicals then went in opposite directions before Pattaya. It may be unfair to label (libel?) them by age or geography, but it seems that some younger men who live or work in more deprived communities stimulated those with a concern for the social dimension to expect a developing integration of the social with the evangelistic as the Lausanne process moved on. Others, perhaps including some of the older leaders in the evangelical circle and emanating more from North America, took fright at what they saw as the watering down of Lausanne's evangelistic concern. Whether the tight structure of the Pattaya gathering was simply because of its methodological agenda, or whether the organisers were concerned to stop the social issue from getting out of hand, is still debated; undoubtedly there were those who felt that Pattaya backed away from the social commitment of the Lausanne Covenant, to the extent that a strongly worded document circulated unofficially at Pattaya on the issue.

The purpose here is not to tell all the history in detail, but simply to illustrate the stresses and strains which affect every part of the worldwide Christian church when we begin to examine God's agenda for that church, and to give an approximate map of where different groups find themselves as they grapple with it. Melbourne and Pattaya are both fading into the past and several developments have already taken place among the groups represented at both; the two conferences simply serve to highlight the intensity with which serious followers of Jesus are facing up to their calling.

Certainly among evangelicals, a fairly heated debate continues. It is symptomatic of the speed at which their debate has proceeded that when one of the greatest of recent evangelical leaders on the world scene – and also one of the most thoughtful and intellectually flexible – Dr John Stott, produced his book *Christian Mission in the Modern World*[13] in 1975, after Lausanne, he had given it in lecture form without undue upheaval in more than one evangelical setting. Yet on the one hand it strongly asserted the need for social action, which would have been considered 'unsound' by some not long before, and on the other it treated evangelism and social action as both good but in essentially watertight compartments of Christian obligation. This would be sharply challenged before long as an inadequate expression of their relationship. While such a clear distinction would be both a concern of Dr Stott's own passion for clarity and a reaction to the hazy use of terms in WCC circles – he quotes Dr Philip Potter telling the WCC Central Committee in 1967, 'ecumenical literature since Amsterdam has used "mission", "witness" and "evangelism" interchangeably'[14] – his concern to keep evangelism on the agenda uncompromised seems to lead him to overstate the case. He did at that stage acknowledge a shift in his position from one in which he would read the Great Commission of Jesus in purely evangelistic terms to a much wider one:

> It is not just that the commission includes a duty to teach converts everything Jesus had previously commanded (Matthew 28.20), and that social responsibility is among the things which Jesus commanded. I now see more clearly that not only the consequences of the commission but the actual commission itself must be understood to include social as well as evangelistic responsibility, unless we are to be guilty of distorting the words of Jesus.[15]

As we have seen, that point can be reinforced if we look at the version of Jesus' commission in Acts 1 and ask what it means to 'be my witnesses'.

Having said this, however, Dr Stott proceeds to look at the relationship between evangelism and social action, and having rightly dismissed social action as either a means to evangelism or a manifestation of it (although in some ways it will always be both), he then concludes that social action should rightly be *a partner of evangelism*. 'Each stands on its own feet in its own right alongside the other,' he says.[16]

The difficulty with this view is that the Jewish mind through which the gospel comes to us simply does not see life in compartments; man is one, and he needs to receive one undivided ministry from God through his people so that the one salvation he receives brings him not only into relationship with God – which is totally pivotal – but brings him the accompaniments of that new life in emotional, material or circumstantial ways. These must be seen *not* as by-products which can readily be set aside as optional extras but as integral parts of the wholeness which God is wanting to give. Certainly all that cannot, in practice, happen in every life, and to that extent the integrated view is only conceptual, notional, perhaps ideal; yet if it is *theologically* valid, it affects our perceptions in a vital way. Instead of the evangelist feeling free to say, 'Well, this man has the bit that really matters, we must do something about the rest if we get time', or 'Now we've evangelised him we can hand him over to the social department,' we are *required* to say 'This man has begun to lay hold on his inheritance in Christ and we simply cannot rest until it is complete; there is something integral missing in terms of God's will and plan for him, and we must bring it into his life.' Such a view helps us to avoid both the abdication and the spiritualising which are common to Christians in the field if we affirm that evangelism and social action may or should be seen as distinct forever. Certainly one of Dr Stott's stature and heart would affirm the morally imperative link between the two; but it is better made if there are not two, but one with a complex of parts.

It is for these reasons that we should not go along with him when he speaks, for example, of the economic and political aspects of the Old Testament concept of *shalom* and then plays them down by saying the New Testament fulfilment '*transcends* the categories in which the promises were given'.[17]

The bald statement is true, but it sidesteps the question, 'Does this transcending then include or exclude the things transcended?' Evangelical interpretation has generally, though unconsciously, *excluded* them and got on talking about the spiritual aspects; if what we have seen in the ministry of Jesus has been rightly seen, then he wanted these things *included* in the greater and newer transcending reality which he was inaugurating. Dr Stott asks, 'Can it be maintained, as serious biblical exegesis, that the New Testament authors present Jesus Christ as winning this kind of peace and as bestowing it on society as a whole?'[18] No, surely not bestowing it fully then and there; but we have been trying in this book to tackle a question which evangelicals have generally not asked, namely 'Do the New Testament authors present Jesus as *wanting* that kind of peace, acting towards it, and expecting his followers to work for it too?' We can quickly agree with Dr Stott when he says,

And there are many Jesuses abroad today. There is Jesus the Bultmannian myth and Jesus the revolutionary fire-brand, Jesus the failed superstar and Jesus the circus clown. It is over against these human reinterpretations that we need urgently to recover and reinstate the authentic Jesus, the Jesus of history who is the Jesus of Scripture.[19]

We need to add, however, that there is also a Jesus of evangelical tradition, a spiritualised Jesus, who similarly needs to be corrected by the perspective of scripture, earthed in our thinking and incarnated in our discipleship.

In a rapidly moving debate it is perhaps unfair to pull to pieces a book published more than a decade ago. We have looked at *Christian Mission in the Modern World* precisely because it was such an honest attempt to tackle the issues, and because even now it represents a position which many of the world's evangelical Christians have not reached in their thinking. In the maelstrom of discussion after Lausanne and Pattaya Dr Stott has also moved on, linking up at one point with a view which prefers to speak of a marriage between evangelism and social action rather than a partnership – an image of closer union than the latter. The positions continue to be formulated. In a way Lausanne was thinking of two boiled eggs in adjacent eggcups, and the 'marriage' thinking envisages two fried eggs in a pan with their whites mingling and their egg yokes remaining intact. I suspect the Bible teaches an omelette.

Dr Stott has given us his own fresh formulation in *Issues Facing Christians Today*.[20] Here he suggests that evangelical Christians have landed up in a limited theological position because their views of God, man, Christ, salvation and the church were all too narrow. Pushing each outwards to its full biblical breadth restores our social witness to its proper place. He concludes:

> Instead of seeking to evade our social responsibility, we need to open our ears and listen to the voice of him who calls his people in every age to go out into the lost and lonely world (as he did), in order to live and love, to witness and serve, like him and for him. For that is 'mission'. Mission is our human response to the divine commission. It is a whole Christian lifestyle, including both evangelism and social responsibility, dominated by the conviction that Christ sends us out into the world as the Father sent him into the world, and that into the world we must therefore go – to live and serve, suffer and die for him.[21]

What, though, of those in the evangelical constituency around the world who oppose even frying the eggs, if not chucking out one of the boiled ones? Let us be clear that it is not their motives which are in question; these are people of God and of prayer, who love those around them and want the best for them. And they see clearly that to feed and clothe and house does not meet all the need of man, for if Genesis is right, he is made for God and lost without him. That, as almost all traditions in the Christian world would agree, was the central question which the ministry of Jesus Christ was to address; even if we look to the gospel records rather than to the more overtly doctrinal material of the epistles, we can make no sense of much of what Jesus said or did without this. And in a world where theologians and ideologists appear with much noise to be denying that, there is no surprise in the depth of feeling with which many want to reaffirm that centrality and the need for evangelism, defined as announcing the news of Jesus with a view to evoking a personal response of faith from the hearer, as a vital means of bringing that ministry of Jesus to good and current effect. This is why – whatever exactly was meant – the Lausanne Covenant in section 6 was drafted to say, 'In the church's mission of sacrificial service evangelism is primary.'

What then, are the grounds for resisting the linking of evangelism to a wider ministry? Some have simply not thought it through. Some have thought it through and frankly do not see social action – beyond a minimal kindness to individuals – as the Bible's teaching. Others fear what will happen because in the past they have seen bodies committed to evangelism trying to widen their ministry and losing the cutting edge of evangelism altogether; that is a well-founded concern. Others again see care as a biblical mandate but hold back when the implications of that caring become structural or political – again, either for fear or on principle or for tactical reasons: 'our missionaries may lose their freedom to preach'. These are not new issues but they can be inhibiting when personal interests, family or a cherished work is at stake.[22]

One particular factor in the discussion is the role played by the so-called Church Growth movement. Pioneered by Dr Donald McGavran of Fuller Theological Seminary at

Pasadena, California, the Church Growth movement has challenged the ineffectiveness of the churches at large in keeping pace with the burgeoning population of the world in its ministry of evangelising and incorporating people into the church. It has pointed out the theological and practical negativity of the churches, restored confidence in both a basic Christian message and bold means of proclaiming it, and provided an assortment of tactics for getting moving again. No end of churches have been influenced, and many thousands exposed to the love of Christ as a result. However, the concern which many have is that the Church Growth enthusiasts have distorted the gospel in their very keenness to spread it. The 'cutting edge' of evangelism has in many places been so emphasised as to minimise the quality of rounded church life and kingdom activity which should ensue. In particular the concept of 'like to like' evangelism, in which each grouping of Christians aims to win its own cultural peers for Christ because they are more likely to respond if the challenge of Christ is at least made in familiar company, has been criticised as reinforcing cultural, socio-economic and tribal barriers within the resulting church rather than seeing them broken down in Christ. There is a fear that the very effectiveness of the method, with all its North American slickness of package and dynamism of approach, is vitiating the integrity of the product.

The debate between social-liberationist and evangelistic perspectives will go on. Its pervasiveness in today's ecumenical discussion is evident over all the theological bookshelves and conference agendas. One such publication on mission[23] reviewed twelve books; leaving aside five which touch the issue indirectly, the six which deal directly with the evangelism-social action question were by a South American liberation theologian, a North American evangelical ex-missionary, a British ex-missionary currently grappling with inner-city poverty, a Chinese theologian, the General Secretary of the World Council of Churches, and an official commission of the Reformed Ecumenical Synod. The gathering is not untypical.

The view from Azusa Street

When the Pentecostal movement exploded in 1900, it was not a cop-out. One of the most striking features of the reports of its early days is the earnestness about Christian living which both provoked and followed its beginnings. Certainly some parts of the movement were evangelical-to-fundamentalist, even revivalist; certainly some parts were in the downtown distress bracket where spiritual escapism is in constant danger of distorting balanced Christianity. But those who were first involved had their eyes on the joy, the power and the generosity of New Testament church life and only wanted that above all – and at any cost. They did not at first ask God for subjective manifestations, but for the fullness of that first-century life to be received. The way it happened took them as much by surprise as anyone else: deep awareness of the presence of God, forms of prayer they had not experienced, healings and a new commitment to each other's welfare – all of these flowed. There is no doubt that as conflict with their existing denominations broke out, and Pentecostals formed their own churches, so attitudes and doctrines hardened and the package offered became more stylised than the package received. Nor is there any doubt that with the passage of time there have come to be Pentecostal churches as comfortable, conformist and middle-class as any in the west.

But to stop there as many liberationist critics do, would be to caricature. For there is no doubt either that other fruits of Pentecostalism are more interesting. South America is the obvious instance, where the conformism of many of the mainline churches has led the Pentecostals to be a popular movement in every sense – not just widely favoured, nor a religious phenomenon of the people, but more deeply involved with where the people are in every way. They have had the most widespread international involvement in actual day-to-day need, and ministry to it, of any Christian group. They have structures for political protest, economic self-help and social transformation. They are in touch with, and appreciated by, the poor and deprived in a way other churches envy.

In other parts of the world the same phenomenon is less marked, but much more real than its critics imply. The profound common man's knowledge of God which Pentecostal experience can promote is most commonly not a cop-out but a share-in; it promotes love and involvement. More than this, for thirty years the experience and insight of the Pentecostals has been seeping sideways into the older denominations, not least the Roman Catholic Church. In these other churches the much-criticised phenomenon of middle-class spiritual high-life has indeed been part of the effect; but it has been a limited part of the scene, and criticism of it has been as unfair as it has been easy. For where an individual or a local congregation has grasped the Christian tradition of its background at all deeply, charismatic renewal has driven the people deeper and not shallower, further on in to costly incarnational service and sideways out of it. For many it has provoked serious personal involvement in the life of God's kingdom for the first time. For others it has motivated, renovated and incarnated.

In South Africa, charismatic renewal has been widespread, largely no doubt because of the pressures and fears unleashed in this crucible. Undoubtedly the escapists have used this expression of Christian experience to sidestep their social obligation, and the critics have been right. But there have been many, often hidden, who would never have faced the facts at all but for this motivation, and many who would never have passed from fear into action and service and protest without that dynamism. Despite the sneers of the critics, it remains true that if we looked for the two hundred local congregations of every denomination which are most effectively engaged in frontline action for good, for change, for peace and for care of the broken and needy in South Africa (and not necessarily those which make the noisiest headlines), we would find that a surprisingly high proportion of them had been deeply touched and motivated by the influence of charismatic renewal in recent years. When the Spirit of the Lord is upon us, we preach good news to the poor.

The view from Johannesburg

In 1984, Mr P. W. Botha (who was just about to shift from Prime Minister to first Executive State President of South Africa) refused a request from Bishop Desmond Tutu (then Secretary-General of the South African Council of Churches) for a meeting with church leaders. His given reason was that he would only agree when the SACC stopped meddling in politics and returned to their proper sphere of the spiritual. As theology is not Mr Botha's proper sphere one can, I suppose, make allowances; but it should be obvious to any Christian that the Bible sees all God's world as one, and all his people needing God's love in both the spiritual realm and the material, most often through other people's care.

There is probably no society in the world where a clear and rounded vision of the church's job is more needed, nor more difficult to maintain, than South Africa. Her problems are known about, though usually over-simplified, around the world. There is acute economic imbalance, there is inexcusable educational deprivation, there are racist laws and attitudes, there are minimal human rights, there are grossly inhuman practices in detention and relocation. There is a legacy of bitterness from ancient conflicts between white and black, between black and black and between Briton and Boer. There is an overwhelming military, a ruthless police and a parasitic and ideologically motivated bureaucracy. And woven in, there are everyone else's social problems of crime and violence, greed and lust, hatred and exploitation. There are embattled ethnic minorities, a self-regarding oligarchy, an attractive parcel of land, and nuclear weapons.

In among all this, there are Christians galore with more inherited theologies than front teeth. The Afrikaners have a Dutch-Calvinist background which combines reverence and personal virtue with a massive construct of theological justification for apartheid, now no longer expounded but alive and well in the folk-memory of the nation. There is ferment in their theology and ecclesiastical structures as that construct is challenged by the young, the brave and the biblical. Young Afrikanerdom sees through the ideology and opts for either a fresh and costly Christlikeness or, more commonly, a tough secularity quite new to his people, toughened by military training and ruthless without its inherited ethic. The white minority, which is polyglot but largely of English and Scottish descent, is caught in between. Their economy, their skins and their conventions pull them into alignment with the Afrikaans community, yet language and history hold them apart, and shared factors push them into direct opposition. Their churches – primarily Anglican, Methodist, Presbyterian and Roman Catholic – have tended both to sanctify their social attitudes and to confront the theological ideology of Afrikanerdom. These churches have not spoken with one voice, but they have been forced more than in some parts of the world to work at the socio-political thrust of the gospel. They have all embraced a large membership of black people, and so have held large groups of people whose suffering and deprivation has been largely at the hands of fellow churchmen. Indeed in this largely Christian society, where 77% still claim to be Christian, only 12% of the membership of the churches is white. The stresses caused by that have been neatly split off in the Dutch Reformed Church through the device of mission churches for the different race groups – at least until recent pressure for 'union'. The Anglican, Methodist, Presbyterian and Catholic churches (among others) have developed an unusual place in the life of South African society just because they have been at once a sheltering place for the downtrodden and an irritant for the middle class. While ministering to the English-speaking sector of the white community, they have been pressed to challenge the very social framework in which they find security. Small wonder that many find it all so uncomfortable that they leave the church; but small wonder too that among black people the westernised style of those churches' life, liturgies and orders can appear anything from welcome to tolerable to wholly alien. The flowering of African Independent Churches (3,000 of them at the last count), colourfully heterodox and vividly indigenous is one cultural reaction to the westernness of the others.

The black community itself is four times the size of the white and so diverse in age, language and political activities that to generalise is foolish. There are still those whose collusion with the South African economic system is both total and voluntary – to earn a living and feed the children is the only goal. There are many whose awareness of the grief and inequity of their situation is acute and immediate, yet who feel helpless to change things and are browbeaten into conformity by the system and the consequences of balking it. And again there are many, especially among students and others who less directly depend on their employer's good will for a living, whose frustrations are unchecked and freely expressed. Particularly in recent years that has led to increasingly frequent outbursts of anger, non-cooperation with officialdom (such as over rent-collection), rioting and other overt resistance. As with the Afrikaner, these younger people are shaking off the forms of faith held by their parents and either dismissing them as irrelevant or insisting that they must be. In some parts of the country this has led to a refreshing if demanding new relevance in the life of the church; in others, to wholesale departure.

It is in this context that the Christian gospel has to make sense in real terms to Simon and Zipho; and in which it has to minister with integrity to both Dorcas and Alice, both Solly and Fanie. It is here that the voice of Bishop Desmond Tutu, humanly passionate and theologically aware, is heard:

African and Black Theology must be concerned – and vitally concerned – with liberation because liberation is a serious preoccupation at the present time, and it is not seen as being an alternative to personal salvation in Jesus Christ. No, it is seen in Africa as the inescapable consequence of taking the gospel of Jesus Christ seriously. Only a spiritually, politically, socially and economically free Africa, where Christianity today is expanding faster than anywhere else in the world, can make a distinctive contribution to the life of the body of Jesus Christ and to the world community as a whole . . .

Black theology arises in a context of Black suffering at the hands of rampant white racism. And consequently, Black Theology is much concerned to make sense theologically of the Black Experience whose main ingredient is Black suffering, in the light of God's revelation of Himself in the Man, Jesus Christ. It is concerned with the significance of Black Existence, with liberation, with the meaning of reconciliation, with humanisation, with forgiveness. It is much more aggressive and abrasive in its assertions, because of a burning and evangelistic zeal, as it must convert the Black man out of the stupor of his subservience and obsequiousness, to the acceptance of the thrilling and demanding responsibility of full human personhood, to make him reach out to the glorious liberty of the sons of God. It burns to awaken the white man to the degradation into which he has fallen by dehumanising the

Black man, and so it is concerned with the liberation of the oppressor equally as with that of the oppressed. It is not so naive as to think that only economic or political oppression are what matter. But liberation must thus be understood in a total sense as removal of all that which keeps us in bondage, all that which makes us less than what God intended us to be.[24]

8 FROM THE PRIORITIES TO THE AGENDA

Dorcas Selele is sitting on the floor, rocking to and fro, face impassive as she grieves. Her friends sit with Dorcas as they surround her daughter, stunned and weeping on the rusted bed. Her teenage girl, Mary, was sitting last night by the untarred street where the open drain has scored a path past the house, when a group of men, migrant workers whose families live two hundred miles away, approached her. They had come from the shebeen, the local drinking house; and when she refused their advances she was stabbed to death and left in her blood in the drain.

The young minister stepped into the room, quietly leaving a bag of food by the door, and sat by the grieving mother, head bowed in pain, arm around her heaving shoulders. He had just come from one of their regular united ministers' meetings with the town council, trying to bring pressure to bear on the authorities to accelerate the improvement of the community. This very area, he had heard, was soon to be developed – streetlights, drains, tarred roads, new housing, unheard-of facilities which many would never see. And the family's house would be flattened to make way for it. The town council was setting up their own police to stop this kind of thing: but what if they too ran out of control? He led a simple prayer in Tswana, relieved that God was so real to these unbroken people in their broken surroundings. Then he sat by Dorcas on the floor, rocking to and fro, young white face impassive as he grieved.

Alice was not in pain, thanks to the skilful handling of

her drugs in the costly private clinic where she lay; but the disease had been taking its course and her life had only hours to run. The young black man by the bed held flowers in his hand, and said Simon was on his way, he had just been held up and asked Zipho to go on ahead. When Simon arrived and asked her forgiveness for the hardness and anger of his feelings in recent months, she somehow knew she was touching a depth of relating, both with him and in what she saw between him and his friend, that was foreign to her superficial knowledge of life. Her other children simply could not handle the situation, shot through as it was with guilt and deceit as well as with sickness and the fragrance of death. Simon, suddenly, seemed to be real and able to cope just where they were artificial and uncomfortable. They could only feel at home in the real world outside the hospital where such oddities as weeping and dying are kept out of sight. Simon meanwhile had encountered a real world in which suffering could be faced and relieved, broken relationships addressed and restored, truth faced, spiritual values perceived and embraced, materialism shrugged off and people known and loved as human beings. It was a place called the kingdom of God, through a gate called self-knowledge and faith; and Alice had so nearly found it when she died.

The new rector of St Agnes' was middle-aged, gracious and wise. Yet there seemed to be a striving, a stretching and a slight sense of threat at his approach. He talked of 'pushing out the boundaries' – the boundaries of Christian maturity, the priorities of God's kingdom, the areas of ministry, the mental recognition of situations often overlooked. It was music to the ears of the young and the committed who sensed, if they did not comprehend, the closed-in structure of the parish's mentality: it was worrying to those for whom the church was a rock in the storm, a lych gate into tranquillity for the emotionally or politically flustered soul. South Africa was too disturbing a place to them and the ivy-clad bricks of

the church made one of the few remaining havens of security
in the turmoil of conscience and self-interest, of goodwill and
dismay in which those people lived.

This book will be useless and theoretical unless we grapple
with what is involved in living out the priorities of Jesus in
the lives of individual Christians and local congregations, as
well as on the wider ecumenical scene; so let us take St Agnes'
as a case study – one of the other churches would have done
just as well – in which to look at the challenges which face
these Christian people, eager and fearful, as they go forward.

Worshipping

The first boundary which needs pushing out is the spiritual
one. It was when Simon came to faith, to a personal knowledge of God, that all his other perspectives and motives
began to change. It was in worship that Corybantic Chapel
could hear the prophetic word of more serious social
involvement. It was in prayer that Jesus chose his disciples,
secured his priorities and faced up to his death. It was at
worship that he gave out his Luke 4 blueprint. We may look
at his priorities in ministry, but miss them entirely unless we
see his first priority of all – keeping at one with his heavenly
Father. 'I do nothing on my own but speak just what the
Father has taught me . . . for I always do what pleases him',
he would say.[1] The Christian who doesn't know God doesn't
know anything.

In the first place, then, St Agnes' needed to look to its
worship. There could be no offering to God of the same old
hymns in the same old way. To enter the gates should be to
enter a corporate encounter with God: one for which leaders
and people had been praying, one whose music and prayers
fitted its theme, one whose warmth of love in the congregation would far transcend the cold individualism of the past. It
needed reverence with joy, eternal verities with immediate

relevance. God on high prompting action on the street. That might need notable changes in the music, the preaching, the furniture, the topics prayed for – even the introduction of the peace at communion, with each moving round to greet his neighbours in Christ. It might mean praying not only for the police, but for the man in the newspaper who was shot by them on Friday. It might mean praying not only for racial harmony, but for the repeal of the Group Areas Act. It might mean learning hymns or choruses in Zulu for a flavour of the worship of the greater body of Christ, or for a planned multiracial service.

It meant, too, that individuals needed to get nearer to God. Simply to congregate once a week, or more likely once a month or so, is not to know God. There needs to be a daily exposure of the Christian's life to God in praise and thanks, Bible study and prayer; when God has invited us into his friendship, a day without that is a day down the drain. The encounter will link with house-group fellowship and public worship; but it must exist at the personal level. At this point the Pentecostals' influence may come in, for their stress on the power of God released into minds and hearts by the Spirit is life-transforming. So much of our preaching has seen God the Father as far up in the heavens and God the Son as far back in history with no immediate contact with us. But God the Spirit of Jesus has been poured into the world since only ten days after the risen Jesus left it – and his delight is to enter and flavour the life of every believer in Christ: 'if the Spirit of him who raised Jesus from the dead *is living in you*, he who raised Christ from the dead will also give life to your mortal bodies through his Spirit, *who lives in you*'.[2] The guarantee of our future resurrection is in our present transformation by that inner residing power, God's Spirit. If that is true, it needs to be so much more existential – something we know as we go along, as a daily encounter with the power and healing love of God planted in us as our birthright from above. All this can be a holy cop-out, but if so it is distorted: for the more we travel towards God, the more he welcomes us in face-to-face embrace and then turns us round by the shoulders to look through his eyes at his world. Then he sends us back, burning with the care of his heart for a world in need; even then, he equips us with more than our own compassion reinforced, but rather with the dynamism of his own heart planted in ours. That is why the individual's encounter with the Spirit is so fundamental to the healing of the world, and why the Pentecostal and the liberationist need to meet.

This, of course, is where the Corybantic Chapel is struggling. Its members have come, as so often happens, from a group of seemingly 'dead' churches in which worship and spiritual life were at a low ebb. They have found a new dynamic in the power of God: some feel as if God had washed, or else electrified, their inner being. Others have found a new language for prayer and praise welling up in their beings. They find the freer format of worship refreshing: choruses, clapping, moving about. They are right. But the more authentic the experience is, the sooner will come the moment when one of the 'words from the Lord' – in a sermon, a tongue, a vision or what-have-you – will have to do with carrying God's love to the poor. One of the most charismatic meetings I have been to included the linking of Jesus' example of humble and costly service in Philippians 2 with a vision of the Christians present going from the brightly lit room where they were, down a set of dark cellar steps to bring the light of Christ which they enjoyed to those in the gloom below. The result, in a nutshell, was a shift in parish policy to reach a dockland flat-dwelling community more effectively, with several of the people giving up flats or houses in more pleasant parts of town to become engaged with the needy and downcast of that area. Just as the Spirit coming on Mary led to the incarnation of Jesus in the heart of Galilee, so a true Pentecost upon the church leads to deeper involvement in the coalface of human need in today's world. When Corybantic hears that word it will struggle between clapping its tambourine into irrelevance and entering the fray more effectively with costly love for the needy. St Agnes', meanwhile, had both a frustrated social programme which needed motivation by God's love on the one hand, and a reluctance to open its life to the charismatic freedom which could release that motivation on the other.

The worshipping boundary needs to be addressed in another way. Alvin Toffler has provided a classic treatment of the culture shock which people undergo when overexposed to rapid change in his book entitled *Future Shock*. One of his shrewd observations is that when people are battling with the culture shock of moving house or country, or when they are having to manage their response to unusually rapid personal or social change, they will tend to create refuges of stability into which they can retreat to a feeling of how it was in the good old days. Some turn their home or their favourite club into a kind of museum where this tranquillity can be experienced. Unfortunately, though entirely naturally, the church is an obvious candidate for that treatment. It claims anyway to represent certain unchanging realities in which man can find security, and so easily the furniture is also rendered unchanging to reinforce the deeper things. The effect is to give the local church a far more tenacious interest in the conservation of liturgies, decorations, and practices than society at large experiences. Churches often feel like last Sunday's flowers just because they cannot throw anything away; congregations become more inveterate hoarders of habits and ways and behaviours than their members are of old golfing hats and corduroy jackets. Change for its own sake has no value; but change for God's sake hits undue opposition for this reason.

Worship hits a cultural boundary at this point. The missionaries who imported Christianity into the colonial world of the nineteenth century imported a good deal of

European culture with it. As we have seen, that culture was likely to be highly tenacious, especially when expatriate Englishmen were using the Anglican Church as a museum of Englishness in the culture shock of foreign climes, as Scots were (and are) doing with the Presbyterian, Irish with the Catholic, and so on. The Dutch Reformed Church still uses middle-Europe architecture. It is just at this point that deprivation occurs, because the wealth of local cultures in Asia, Africa or South America could enrich the life and worship of the churches beyond anything they knew 'at home'; yet it is just there that the resistance to changing what is remembered (even in the third generation of immigration) is greatest. 'African music is one of the richest art forms in the world',[3] yet many of the churches imported into Africa don't know it. In Alexandra parish the new hymn board has five columns so the English hymns translated by the missionaries into Zulu, Xhosa, Tswana and Sotho can all be sung to the same nineteenth-century British tunes: the effect is marginally more of Pentecost than of Babel, but where are the indigenous hymns and African instruments, marimbas, harps and drums? Those songs *are* sung, not least at the twenty-minute 'peace'; but at other times the freedom to enjoy local music is nearly as inhibited as at St Agnes'. Yet it is St Agnes', in the 'white' parish, which most needs the marimbas – both to enrich its monocultural worship experience and to open up the experience of being part of 'the whole body, joined and held together by every supporting ligament (which) grows and builds itself up in love, as each part does its work'.[4] Not to know what each part is doing, even broadly, is not to know the fullness of worship. The New Testament gives us a hymn from heaven which worships Christ as the lamb of God in these words: 'You are worthy . . . because you were slain, and with your blood you purchased men for God from every tribe and language and people and nation. You have made them to be a kingdom and priests to serve our God.'[5] To be without at least some awareness of those tribes and languages and nations, especially when we live cheek by jowl with them, is to impoverish our whole Christian experience – and not least in worship when we encircle the throne and sing the lamb's new song. It is good that South Americans use ponchos for vestments, but sad to see cassocks and surplices in equatorial Africa. It is enriching to feel the flow of music and language and prayer from our neighbour Christians pulsing in the wineskins of our own tradition. West Indian music is needed in the Church of England for that reason – not as a gimmick but as a means of showing it the multi-faceted richness of being the body of Christ in Britain. And so on. The Dutch Reformed Church, in its determination to have worship for its 'own culture' is losing at the very point where it thinks it is rich; in practice most of us do the same. The fear of ecumenical progress in many places is rooted in the fear of losing one's own ecclesiastical identity, one's style of doing and being; yet it is not until that particular corn of wheat falls into the ground and dies that the ever-new ear of the full corn of God grows up for all to enjoy.

One corollary of this is that if the worship of the church is utterly culturally alien to the one in which it is offered, that community will not relate to it and may never enter into worship at all. That has been the church's experience (and fault) in many parts of the world. It can easily apply in inner-city Britain, where the essentially bookish and cerebral format of middle-class liturgies cuts no ice at all; and the only way ahead is to freshen up the format in the style of local life. But if the minister is himself a product of an outside culture, and especially if he needs to take refuge in the forms of the church as a refuge from the culture shock of the community where he is working, he will all the more disqualify his ministry from making the cultural leap that is needed. And all sorts of doors, not least the trap door between man and his God, will stay closed.

Growing up

Paul declared it as the aim of his ministry to present every-one mature in Christ.[6] In the cerebral west we can slip into thinking that this means having a mature intellectual knowledge of our faith, so we lay on a course to fix it. But in fact it has to do with a greater maturity, a growth towards both understanding and the knowledge of God, to both Christlike character and Christlike goals of service. Before we can reach the point when Christians come to exercise a rounded ministry in all the dimensions which match the work of Jesus, they need to see that rounded vision, want that rounded lifestyle, and embrace that rounded calling. That will be maturity; for the church, it will be when everyone is at it together in a shared vision and a common work – when 'the whole body, joined and held together by every supporting ligament, grows . . .' This is the second boundary we must push at.

For this there must be teaching. We have seen how readily we all perceive our Christian calling through blinkers (p. 150). While there are spiritual factors keeping the blinkers on – the cost of taking them off, the devil's vested interest in keeping them on – our mental perceptions have a lot to do with it. A visit to St Agnes' once a month for communion with a three-minute exhortation to try harder, based loosely on the gospel reading, is likely to be less than life-transforming. In the well-known catchphrase, 'sermonettes make Christianettes'. We need to budget for an extensive, balanced, systematic and digestible teaching programme in every local church. We need greater understanding to be given at every service of worship. Even where communion is the rhythm of Sunday morning worship, we need a good sermon, well thought out, well presented, theologically well based – and not too short. We need to encourage 'twicing' – the habit of worship both morning and night, especially when we are growing a church out of immaturity. Often the evening can provide a time of joyful worship less limited by the length of Sunday schools, coupled with a solid time of teaching, a chance to respond before God in prayer, and a time for fellowship to follow. Why not elucidatory questions as the teacher goes along? Why not notebooks, pencils, and an overhead projector, if these help understanding to grow? Too many of our leaders and ministers frustratedly belabour their people for not acting out the gospel's lifestyle when they themselves are at fault in not giving the teaching from which that lifestyle grows.

For most growing churches around the world, some pattern of midweek groups – whether called home groups, house churches, prayer fellowships or what – has been an essential system for fostering that growth in understanding.[7] Theologians of liberation in South America have rightly challenged the western churches for their pride in ortho*doxy* (right belief and right worship) without what they have called ortho*praxis* (right action). Unless we are *doing* the Christian life we are not *believing* rightly.[8] Home churches of this kind need to be a microcosm of the body of Christ, worshipping, studying, interceding, caring for the members and undertaking acts of service and witness in the community. These are what Howard Snyder calls 'kingdom tasks'. One of our ladies' groups visits the residents of an old people's home, another used to make frozen meals for girls coming home from the maternity ward, another will form a work party to serve a poor community. Our groups visit Alexandra by rotation for worship on Sunday morning, as much to receive the joy and the cultural breadth of the body of Christ as to support, to give, to express multiracial fellowship in a segregated society. It isn't much, but it helps. In fact it is of particular importance because part of our maturing is the renewal of attitudes which we do not even know we hold – of superiority, complacency, racial distaste or whatever. South Africa is designed to keep people from knowing each other, so that prejudice and the laager mentality reinforce each other. We live and react out of images, not realities. So anything which helps us to encounter reality in the flesh, and not via others' opinions or the distorted media, is of value. It enfleshes the Christian response in first-hand awareness. For this reason it is always good to have projects on the go into which ordinary church members can be drawn as helpers (examples below). The fancy word for this is 'contextualising' the gospel – working through the ways in which Christianity can be part of our local social reality, and the ways in which it addresses that reality in compassion or confrontation. That will go nowhere if the people of God are themselves cut off from their context and living with caricatures of it.

This problem, of course, is acute in South Africa where racial prejudice and the Group Areas Act make contact difficult. But in practice most comfortable (and even uncomfortable) Christians in the rest of the world prefer to avoid knowing too much about how others live and what they face – even though these people are their brothers and sisters in Christ. Many British Christians could do with a week in a coalmining village, many Europeans with a week where their cheap labour comes from, many North Americans with a week in the *favelas* around the great cities of South America. The holiday funds spent getting to Europe could sometimes be more Christianly spent in understanding Liverpool, Lebanon, Burma or Lichtenburg – that is, the Lichtenburg in the western Transvaal which is a centre of both conservative white South African farmers and the government's ruthless relocations policy. All of this pushes out the boundary of growing understanding.

There is often a place in today's church for a study course in addition. The hunger for Christian knowledge is so widespread that many churches have found a market for courses on doctrine, the Bible, church history or Christian living. The only danger is 'studyitis' – the practice of adding ever more head knowledge without working it out in life. For that reason a church with a regular study programme needs to put in a directly service-orientated course every so often (on, say, counselling or socio-economic issues which can be tackled). It is also good to orientate the homework assignments in that direction – not 'What does Paul say about the lordship of Christ' but 'Produce a Sunday school lesson on . . .' or 'Make a plan to implement the lordship of Christ in a specific area of your life before Christmas.'

Here again the contextual will be ducked if we do not plan to face it head-on. It is so much easier to learn, and even to express, new depths of our faith in our own socio-cultural framework than to bridge the gulfs and break down the barriers with it. Fit young people can be set to work things out in a hospital – perhaps as nursing auxiliaries in a school or college holiday. Middle-class suburbanites need exposure to inner-city life and the industrial process; else they simply have no perception of what others are contending with. Dominant groups in society very rarely enter the setting of downtrodden or minority groups: white Americans need to interface with American Indians, high-caste Indians and Pakistanis with the lower castes, Chilean city-dwellers with the Indians of the Chaco, Northern Irish Protestants with local Roman Catholics, Christian Kikuyu with other Kenyan tribes, and so on to the Afrikaner with the baSotho. There is no other way to mean what we say about the body of Christ, or about the lordship of Christ going beyond our other loyalties. And there is no other way to understand where either our brothers or our sisters are so that we can begin to love them as we are told to.

Language is pivotal here. Many in the west have no idea just how complex the language picture is in much of the Third World, nor how effectively it divides people up and shuts them in to themselves. Imposed language is deeply resented, and experiments with such imposition have back-fired in several countries – not only in South Africa, where the requirement of several subjects to be learned in Afrikaans as a medium of instruction in Soweto schools was the final flash point for the 1976 riots. People identify deeply with their language (the Welsh as much as the Afrikaners) and there is ultimately no way to penetrate other people's thought-worlds but to learn their language. That can be a hard and tedious exercise, though its fruits in openness from friends and perception of their culture are worth every bit. Even without that, it is the costly path of love which leads to growth and unity in the body of Christ: and at times there is no other way. So as we plan to grow, not only in ourselves or our comprehension but in our usefulness to God's kingdom and our brothers in Christ's body, we may need to earmark a holiday or a year's correspondence course to get inside another's language in this way. That could apply as much to British youngsters who want to evangelise on the holiday beaches of Spain as to others in more complex linguistic situations. I know one man in Africa who very haltingly preached in the vernacular at a service and was later told by a sister in a religious order that English missionary sisters had spent half their lives in her country and still could not say 'Good morning' in the local language: her eyes stood full of tears as she set the care of the one against the disdain of the other.

At St Agnes', some of the young would take that seriously as they have already been exposed to black people and know how embarrassing it is to have not even a greeting for their fellow believers. They are already being trained in Christian living by the new rector's Sunday programme, coupled with the exposure to ministry into which he is leading them in various places of need. Bridleway Baptist is a little threatened by their Anglican neighbour, for they have been running Bible courses for years and have some of the 'best taught' Christians in the locality. Their unease arises because the St Agnes' people are *doing* more on the wings of their learning; and thank God they have the humility to ask if they can come in on some of the projects and learn. They had followed Jesus' example of teaching in the synagogue, but forgotten that he also did it in the fields and the highways where the hungry, the sick and the broken were blessed and the disciples taught about service.

Caring

To Emmanuel's activist minister, all of this looks rather tame. He perhaps forgets just how many sound barriers of the spirit he and his congregation have passed through over the years to reach the place where they are now. Worshipping beside other race groups in the same pew took some getting used to, especially with a sermon interpreted every week into a second (and sometimes a third) language. Nipping in and out of officially forbidden areas comes naturally – but didn't always. Realising the security police had an informer in the congregation was hard until they decided to do God's thing regardless. These very sound barriers hold back the folk at St Agnes' and at Bridleway, as well as at the Corybantic Chapel – and the Dutch Reformed Church is miles behind; indeed half the time they are preaching the barriers up more than pulling them down. But we must tackle the boundary of compassion where it is limiting us now, rather than where we wish it was.

One of the biggest dangers is that Emmanuel may despise acts of care by the others on the grounds that our society is in such a mess that only structural change can put it right. It is sometimes said that the church delays revolutionary change by its Band-Aid ministry, which patches up the hurts without addressing the causes and rooting out the disease underneath. Indeed it is said, if the church only stopped those things the position might become acute enough for the poor to rise up and demand their rights and freedoms.

We will see further on that the churches are certainly not allowed to do charitable things as an alternative to seeking justice by structural means. But they have to go on doing Band-Aid jobs when exclusively political movements might contemptuously stop. The chief reason is that Jesus, in a radically oppressive situation, went on caring for individuals one by one in a personal Band-Aid way, and commanded us to do likewise in his name. Among other reasons is the fact that structural change is too big and complex a matter to be guaranteed, least of all by our stopping caring; we simply cannot ask the needy to pay that price. It becomes like the communist practice of announcing that all will be well at the end of a five-year plan if everyone works for that plan in the meantime; but somehow the benefits never arrive. So the churches have to work at individual care in the context of a continuing pursuit of social justice at the bigger level; the balance of the ministry of Jesus directly compels us.

Specifics are difficult now, because each society is so different in the detail of human need and how it is met. At St Agnes', there are two clear sets of needs: those in the immediate community, and those arising from the peculiarities of South Africa. The first set are fairly universal. There are lonely older people who can be visited at home, given lifts to church, invited to a meal. An apparently ordinary midweek service with tea to follow and a lift each way is a major focal point for some who live alone. Sunday's worship and sermon (not just the sermon!) can be recorded and the housebound equipped with a cassette player to hear it during the week, and feel part of the bigger congregation. Young people really do need social centres, Christian teaching and personal guidance. Creches, Sunday schools and youth groups matter. So do marriage preparation, hospital visits, caringly conducted funerals: and into much of it the whole congregation can be gradually drawn to serve. The same applies in the healing ministry, where many can be helped to pray with the sick, the anxious, the guilty and the uncommitted to counsel them and to help them find release.

The issues arising peculiarly from South Africa may illustrate at least the principles of what can be done elsewhere. For example, most white South Africans who employ domestic workers treat some or all of Thursday as a day off. Many churches run a 'Centre of Concern' on that day at which skills in literacy, needlework, typing or cooking are taught. Inevitably there is the criticism that this merely produces more useful slaves for the whites; but as mainly Christian venues, they can be a valuable place to meet friends without being moved on, an opportunity for song and prayer, and a real chance to learn skills which help women to cope for themselves (can you imagine visiting the supermarket and not being able to read the labels on the tins?) and to provide for their families by sewing school clothes or knitting things for sale. It's not much, but it's something – especially as several centres act as employment agencies, and one even runs a dental clinic.

Or take the soup. A few years ago the wife of a clergyman noticed the conditions under which Sowetans fetch their pensions (described in chapter one). Our own church now sends a team every second month with enough soup and bread for over 3,000 women one day and half that number of men the next, and distributes it jointly with friends from a Soweto parish. Nutritionally it is next to nothing, but in winter it is welcome, it is always a change from waiting, and the multiracial team doing the work is a sign of something God is doing. After the soup a hand is given with getting the very elderly, the handicapped and the sick to the necessary tables to sort things out; sometimes people need to be carried, sometimes the officials can be encouraged to cooperate, sometimes an errand can be run or someone who collapses be taken to hospital. Last time I was there a young woman who had suffered a stroke and lost the use of her legs was having trouble climbing a slope, and my wife Gill came to find me. I was with the rector of the Soweto parish, and we joined our hands in a first-aid clasp and carried her with an arm round each of our necks. Again it was a little thing – until I caught Jacob's eye and we both grinned as we realised what was happening in a simple act of service: the clasping of black hands and white hands would ease one of Africa's hurts. It isn't much; but it is something – perhaps more than can be done from the correspondence columns of a Washington newspaper. And it's a sign of the kingdom.

Then there was a drought. South Africa has been, with most of the region, in the grip of the worst drought for 200 years. In the western Transvaal there are both poor rural communities and relocation areas – barren patches of land in which the government has set up toilets and dumped numbers of unwanted people from other areas. The whole business is a horror story of deceit and brute force, land deprivation and unspeakable hardness of heart. The impossibility of either growing food or finding employment in many of these areas has earned the policy the name of creeping genocide. There are other areas, but our church decided to focus on just this one; in 1983 it sent several trucks of food and clothing and enough cash to buy a two-ton truck and buy maize meal – the staple diet – in bulk for sale at cost in distant communities. There were handouts for the destitute but dignity was preserved, without the usual rip-off, for most. A sewing centre and a candle-making works were set up by the people on the spot. In 1984 the cash went on but teams of city Christians began spending weekends in these remote areas, the women and children packing and distributing food boxes and the men helping to build a church as both a worship and community centre. Again it isn't much, but when it involves two four-hour drives, two nights on the floor and sheer hard work, it is more than nothing. And, of course, when South Africa's blacks see white people kneeling at their feet with soup, or mixing concrete with their sons, or drinking the same brown water which is all they can dig from the river, it is a sign of the kingdom. The ways of the world have been challenged, and the dominant white has been seen as a servant: not much, but something.

In other parts of the country Christian people are engaged in founding a clinic in the Crossroads squatter camp, in finding building materials for destitute relocated people in the Orange Free State, in setting up water supplies, combating disease and initiating all kinds of income-bearing craft industries in communities which would otherwise have no access to distant markets. It isn't much, and of course it is no defence for the system. But it is real, it is widespread, and it is a testimony to the love of Jesus which is not misread. It need not be paternalistic or undignifying, nor does it soften the demand for change. In any case it's what Jesus said to do. And it is simple enough that anyone from St Agnes' or anywhere else can find a serving niche without great enterprise, great funds or great time commitment. They just need a bowl and a towel. The same kind of thing can be translated into any community in the world, if that spirit of service for Jesus has been born. And many of these initiatives have begun in just that charismatic environment which is mocked for being a cop-out. God is pushing out the compassion boundary.

Prophesying

Social justice has been an unparalleled bugbear in the life of the Christian church. Some have seen the gospel as entirely addressed to the need for social harmony and have given heart and soul to its pursuits. Others have written off the first group as unspiritual, often needing to be saved! The two have all too often polarised and simply thrown bricks from behind theological stockades – a sad slide from the days when those most open to prayer and evangelism were also most devoted to justice. One forgets that Lord Shaftesbury had 'Come, Lord Jesus' printed on all his stationery; his belief in the imminent coming of Christ was not a cop-out from justice here and now but a mighty incentive to finding it. We have to push out the boundary of the church's pursuit of justice while we are pushing out the others.

St Agnes' was rocked to the roots by what some of South Africa's bishops have had to say to the government. Trevor Huddleston left long enough ago to be known as a hero, but at the time was a troublesome stirrer in the eyes of many. Bridleway has gone one further, beyond the comfortable conformism of the Anglicans, to produce a theology of political quiescence and submission to the powers that be on the basis of Romans 13; it ties in with the Dutch Reformed Church's exegesis. Corybantic started off in a similar place, indeed there was some research to show that worried white people were bolting for the new independent charismatic churches as an escape from the South African facts of life.[9] But unlike some which have simply petered out, these folk have kept listening to God and – so fast does change happen there by comparison with churches more set in their ways – are beginning to hear his challenge to tackle the social issues. Emmanuel, of course, has been in the forefront all along, though sometimes buying ideologies without sieving them through theology.

How does a local church approach the work of challenging injustice in a complex modern state? The individual can do it by joining political bodies and working for good in that field. He can write to the press (not such a sign of madness in South Africa as elsewhere, while the press remains one of the few relatively open channels of protest). He can enter a career which gives him access to influence – as a politician or a lawyer who can take up cases involving known injustices in the system; as a businessman with a say in working conditions, pensions, unionisation and the like; as a writer or broadcaster on social issues which need publicity; perhaps as a medic who can help pick up the pieces. He can object to military service and weaken the conscription machine by being known to have gone to jail for it. He can leave the country and work for pressure from exile. If he chooses he can go the radical route of subversion and training for sabotage. Christian people have followed each of these routes and others.

But how about the local church? It does not have the freedom of the individual, nor is it likely to have such a consensus in the membership that it can act decisively in unity.

The local congregation can, of course, make an impact locally. It tends to have a fair proportion of local people in it. There are probably some who know people of influence in local government, and can talk to them. There are probably good contacts with the high street business owners if it is a matter of not displaying an offensive poster or watching out for teenagers bullying children. They can get up a petition about the use of the park (even de-segregating it), the safety of a bus depot or the poor street lighting on the old people's way home. In some countries (like South Africa) they can agree to a minimum wage which they will give to domestic workers and publicise it in order to shove the other employers' rates upwards. They can (as we do) join up ecumenically to run a courteous and visible Christian bookshop where local people can pop in for Bibles, books, notepaper and a chat; the shop's very presence will affect the tone of the high street, the video shop's publicity, and so on. If they are prepared to serve, they can speed up the opening of a day nursery, an old people's centre or a meals on wheels service just by offering to man it. And of course if something really offensive is happening in the neighbourhood they can publicise, persuade, and if necessary pressurise – for as a body they have both purchasing power and nuisance value if they choose to use it. In our area the evening newspaper delivery used to be done by black men on motor scooters, who were taken off in favour of affluent local teenagers on bicycles. Since the service has been poor ever since there has been good reason for a steady flow of callers from our parish to the newspaper suggesting that they employ some black people again.

Where people abuse the powerless, it is remarkable how much can be done just by a presence. Twice recently white South Africans have come to the defence of blacks on segregated beaches and told the police who were trying to remove them to get lost – and they have. That reflects a new mood in South Africa; it doesn't justify those beaches which are still segregated, but it is new for whites to stand up for blacks in that way. Likewise the presence of the soup team has affected the way petty officials herd up the pensioners. Even a clerical collar in the corner shop affects the way a proprietor speaks to a black customer.

Another effective area is publicity. As Jesus observed, wrong loves the dark, and publicity is a form of light. Most dodgy bureaucracies make things as complicated as possible so the poor client is always unsure of his ground. Certainly South African law does that. So it pays to run articles in the church magazine or the diocesan newspaper which set out clearly what the law is – even if people then conscientiously decide to disobey it – on what a pensioner's rights are or what a policeman is not allowed to do. It can be good to draw the attention of the press to a situation which needs to be opened up.

Then there are public pronouncements. These can be more abrasive than helpful, but where diplomacy has borne no fruit, they can take the lid off an issue. And where something wrong is entrenched, persistent reference to it in public with the reminder that it is immoral is useful. In South Africa the Prohibition of Mixed Marriages Act has gone, Group Areas and influx control may soon change, and migrant labour may be modified so that a working man's family can live

with him. Not Utopia, but progress; and while a new mood
and business pressure have something to do with it, it is
good to believe that the steady dripping of moral criticism
from the churches over nearly forty years is now making its
mark.

Another major area is that of education and research.
We are one of those churches which runs courses such
as described earlier under *Growing up*. A recent one tackled
the issue of living Christianly in South Africa and was
attended by 150 who heard about law, economics, relocations, detention without trial, torture, and the feelings of
South Africa's blacks and Afrikaners. Small groups are
working on various action plans, blacks who came are
encouraged, and many individuals are far more aware of
what is happening round them. Most will never be the
same again.

There is space, particularly, for study and research on the
precise relevance of some of the Bible's social legislation for
our modern societies.[10] What, for example, is the precise
application of the jubilee legislation? How significant is it
that in Israel everyone had some sort of landholding stake in
the nation and that all debts were cancelled every seven
years? That must say something about the pattern of loans
and interest payments in the west. In the Old Testament
'provision for periodic debt remission and the ban on interest
both aim to stop this process at its root by discouraging
lenders from lending'.[11] If the profit motive were reduced in
the finance market, what would be the effects for human
welfare and family life?

One area which cries out for thought is that of family
life – not so much the overworked issues of divorce, abortion
or one-parent families, but the whole issue of the place
of the family as a social building brick. In Israel it was
the answer to loneliness (especially among the elderly), to
social security, to employment, to youth crime and to local
government.

The key problem addressed by the Old Testament Law is how to institutionalize love in human social structures, when Man is recognised as a fallen creature. The world has seen many solutions proposed, in Capitalism and Socialism, by Mao, Marx and Milton Friedman. The God-given solution in the Old Testament, however, lies in the institutions of family and kinship. The imperfections of family and kinship relationships may be many, for Man is fallen, but biblical emphasis on the role of kinship and family suggests no more 'loving' institutional form will be found. Contemporary support for this proposition from non-biblical thinkers is striking, from both sociology and sociobiology.[12]

If not perfect, the extended family has much to commend it in our fragmented world, and there are social means by which its stability and responsibility can be encouraged, not least through the tax and property-owning systems which can presently militate against it. Here the Christian can bring an influence to bear by his family example, by support of family-centred projects in the locality (e.g. building granny flats into houses, running family events on a Sunday), by knowing the case for 'familyism' and organising it in society, and by supporting central government in its favour. That applies with migrant labour in South Africa but in other ways overseas.

Another implication of Israel's social structure is the way central government was limited in favour of local institutions. Influence over one's own life is noticeably greater when decisions are made nearer to one's own local community, by local people for local needs. The centralising trend is strong worldwide, but matched by growing ineffectiveness in an anonymous society, which central authorities know all about. In the end it is in their interest to decentralise and Christians should be pressing for that. The more it happens, the more a local Christian community can act effectively in the interests of local people in the face of avarice, ugliness and inhumanity in the locality. The inability of the central government to sustain the overwhelming scale of increased social security spending in western countries seems likely to force a return to family responsibility and local projects; Christians should be there in the forefront to pick that up as an issue.

Any of our five cartoon churches could pick these issues up if they chose to. Even in the Dutch Reformed Church, many of the pastors and leaders are longing to move away from the South Africa of the past. They need to stand up and be counted; but even without confronting the might of the system, they can achieve immense amounts by the way they preach in the presence of policemen, magistrates, soldiers and businessmen. They have the ears of cabinet ministers, Broederbonders and bureaucrats; they can infect the whole system with humanity and restraint if they choose to.

St Agnes', meanwhile, is full of executives with influence over labour policy, working conditions, pensions, and investment plans; many of those have access to municipal authority and funds for development projects. But their time and effort priorities have to be retrained.

Corybantic, St Agnes' and Bridleway all have a long way to go in what is (uglily) called 'conscientising' their people: that is, making them aware of the situation in which they live, God's view of it, and possible action plans which they could follow. They need to bring their own lives into integrity – not speaking in tongues in church while under-paying their employees or singing the Magnificat while depriving the hungry of good things. They need to face up to the story of the elder in the Apostolic Faith Mission in South Africa who thought it was his Christian duty to cane one of the Mission's black pastors when he was detained by the police. They need to see God's goals for justice and humanity and then look for specific means of moving towards them. When intimidated they need to see that there is so much that can be done before serious confrontation with state authority even begins – and start doing it. But of course they also need to learn that the state can become a beast in the eyes of God (as in Revelation 13) and be more afraid of God than of it. Only that way will they find the courage to confront the authorities when they are disobeying God. They may need assumptions in their doctrine of the state corrected, and the cost of authentic Christian challenge to it set out. Then they will need to learn what Emmanuel has already broadly embraced, that in spite of respect and submission towards authority in its divinely intended role, there is divinely intended conflict which sometimes has to be accepted by the faithful Christian. There is a time to say no to the police, a time to lie down in front of the bulldozers, a time to march in the streets, a time to ask how the just war theory applies to internal affairs. And the track record of the church suggests that the time is often sooner rather than later, for later has so often been too late. That has never been more eloquently put than in the famous words of Martin Niemöller, a church leader under Hitler:

> In Germany they came first for the communists, and I didn't speak up because I wasn't a communist. Then they came for the Jews and I didn't speak up because I wasn't a Jew. Then they came for the trade unionists, and I didn't speak up because I wasn't a trade unionist. Then they came for the Catholics, and I didn't speak up because I was a Protestant. Then they came for me, and by that time no one was left to speak up.

Proclaiming

The main reason Bridleway is nervous of politics is that it seems to threaten the priority of evangelism. People need to know Christ, to be forgiven their sins and brought into the community of God's people and the hope of eternal life: so the present world surely must come second. Corybantic has a similar philosophy, and so – conveniently – has the Dutch Reformed Church. Emmanuel takes precisely the opposite line, seeing evangelism as a spiritualising cop-out from the work of justice. And St Agnes' is so happy about both politics and commitment to Jesus that it won't discuss either at the dinner table . . .

The hesitations are valid. Certainly in South Africa, the roving evangelist with his tent and collection bag is a common phenomenon in every culture; he arrives, preaches, gets people forward, takes up the offering and goes. The intentions of some are worthy and of others mercenary. In most cases there is no follow-up care, no resulting community for fellowship, training, support or Christian service, and no noticeable impact on the bad news of life as it is experienced by the bulk of the people. So the working biblical ministry of evangelism is discredited by some and pushed aside by others. What is worse, the church which has spoken most of the need for evangelism in the past – the Dutch Reformed Church – seems to be interested in freeing people from one set of sins while firmly in the grip of another set itself.

The corrective for abuse is always right use, not non-use. With evangelism this means that we have to work at a valid evangelism which flows from the word of God but operates with integrity in our world. The command to do it is unequivocal if we sit under the authority of the words of Jesus: 'go and make disciples . . . Go . . . and preach the good news . . . You are witnesses . . . As the Father has sent me, I am sending you . . . you will receive power . . . and you will be my witnesses . . . to the ends of the earth'.[13] Some would try to dilute 'be my witnesses' into a very hazy kind of Christian permeation of the atmosphere by God's vaguest of people – but the group who were told to be that did it first of all by talking loudly and clearly about Jesus so that others could embrace his message. They did not fail to do the practical caring, the teaching and worshipping and influencing of society towards justice, but they did clearly and specifically preach the news of Jesus so people would say yes or no to it. That is the fifth boundary.

Those first Christians had the balance right. When they presented Jesus as the Messiah whom the Old Testament foretold and as the one who was handed over to death by the deliberate plan and foreknowledge of God revealed in the scriptures,[14] they knew that he was the answer to all the sin and depravity which the Old Testament had inveighed against. The same prophet who spoke of Jesus as 'led like a sheep to the slaughter' for the sins of men also spoke of us as sheep who have turned to their own way[15] – that was man's problem. And Isaiah, of all the prophets, knew that this 'own way' was not only religious, a matter of idolatry to foreign gods, nor only personal, a matter of immorality, but corporate – a matter of collusion in social injustice. So just as John the Baptist called them to turn from injustice if they wanted the baptism of repentance, so Peter and the other apostles had that in their minds when they went about the near East calling people to repent and be baptised for the forgiveness of their sins.[16]

In our day, then, it will not do to preach Christ only as a saviour from personal naughtiness, though immorality does count with God, nor as a liberator from occult bondage and the worship of falsehood, though he loves to do that too. It is necessary for the repentance we preach to include a turning from social sin, from direct exploitation or oppression of others, and from collusion with institutional evil in our world. Of course, no one can put all of that right at a stroke, but he can turn to God and plead for forgiveness for his association with structures of oppression and acts of evil and set his face as much to fight these things in his Christian life as he will abhor idols and shun adultery.

Anything less does not constitute biblical repentance and does not release divine forgiveness; for God, as we know from Levi, Zacchaeus and Dives, does not look lightly on societal sin.

To fudge evangelism is not only to disobey our Lord Jesus Christ. It is to cut off the supply line of effective Christians in society, for only as people come beyond a nominal membership of the church to a deep and personal awareness of having been released by Christ and brought into linkage with him, will they be equipped to go and change the world in his name. If they have not always done so in the past, it is partly because they were neither evangelised nor taught correctly. If they perceive the obligation to tackle social justice as well as compassion and mercy at the point of their commitment, and are reinforced in that by steady and articulate teaching there will be little difficulty in deploying them in a rounded ministry.

Evangelism, of course, is a sensitive business; Jesus likened it to fishing, which is not the same for salmon as it is for bass or herring. It requires an ability to deal with real people in all their individuality. One of the St Agnes' ladies may have come to faith through discussion with Christian friends while her husband, long involved in and depressed by secular politics, might have come through taking the photographs at a multiracial service and seeing there a vision of unity in care never encountered before. Another may have come as a cynical atheist doctor through seeing his own baby healed of incurable handicaps by the power of God. Another may have come through longing for a richer married life, and only finding it in the forgiveness and trust bestowed by the Lord. Another again may have suffered grave disease and been met by God's care in the hospital. These and others will be in every lively church; and not surprisingly, the church which is most authentically representing Christ across the breadth of its life will most effectively magnetise a wide range of people to them.

Once they meet Christ, of course, the process of rounding must begin – the process of helping the newly converted or revived to reflect the wholeness of Christian discipleship in their personal lives in the fellowship of God's balanced people. Every one will need boundaries of worship and growth, of care and protest and witness pushed out to the fullness of what God wants for them – and each individual, being differently shaped and prejudiced, will need personal help with the growing pains. What is sure is that he can't get it right if his church has it wrong.

Bridleway, then, needs to build up its social involvement if it is to be seen to do the very things it has made so much of teaching. Zipho can write it off as a religious escape, a cerebral Bible-trip unless that orthopraxis comes into view. Its members need to find Dorcas Selele where she is, as a sister in Christ with her own cultural heritage and ways of expressing her devotion. They need to understand the wholeness God plans for her and not only provide the blankets and food and clothing which she needs, but start to tackle the authorities delaying her pension, her re-housing or her vote. The Corybantic Chapel choir will want to sing with her, not for her; to learn her music as much as sing her theirs. They will weep when she is weeping, sit with her at Mary's grave, and make friends as she squats with her children. They will praise God for new drains as well as new tongues, and plead for a new brand of healing.

Emmanuel, too, will open its eyes. For the vision of justice they learned from Isaiah has hardened their hearts to Fanie and Alice; in challenging sin they have bypassed the sinner. The despised Dutch Reformed Church will find friendship extended, a friendship not spoiled by indifference to wrong but inspired by a longing to meet and to speak. No longer the verbal brickbats, but a meeting of minds, a sharing of hearts, a theological encounter between the ministers and a practical love between their fellowships. As trust grows (and criticism for others goes with it) so the sharing of minds and the opening of prejudice can begin. And Fanie is meeting with Zipho through Simon, distrustful but learning to listen, finding a brother and hearing a hurt and seeing a vision his upbringing had never made space for. The myths of their histories can both be despatched in the newness of following as one. Truth can be spoken, perspectives transformed and attitudes broken and made. It is slow, but real; and it percolates out to their families and friends, political attitudes and voting, spending patterns and ways of speaking. And the kingdom of God is there.

Emmanuel also sees the shock of a life transformed. Because Simon and Zipho can speak of their meeting with Christ, and Fanie can witness to Christ setting free his perspectives, the dimension of the Spirit can be taken seriously. It is not the human pressure only, the techniques and policies and protests of man, but the living power of God which undoes such damage as Simon's, such hurt as Zipho's or such blindness as Fanie has been bred in. They all, we all, need setting free at every level of being. And so they will come and pray for Alice as well as querying her wealth; to condemn will no longer be their tool, but to care and set her free into generosity. Before she dies, perhaps, her heart will be opened to Christ, her mind to the world and her purse to the poor. It can be.

For Solly, too, the whole dim history of Christian links with Jews can be changed. For they know they have to share with him the news which they have learnt; but they do it not in strident tones but in the love of God and in the sensitivity which feels his tension and his adolescence, his lack of identity and his fear of rejection. They will draw beside in friendship, set a vision of human unity to transcend the ethnic walls of our cultures, affirm the goodness of his history and yet urge him on to more. To evangelise will be to fulfil, not to deny, all he is; and to convert will be to bind him into the workforce of the kingdom as it builds for healing and justice. Somehow solidarity in the oneness of worship and service, compassion and protest at evil will transcend the loyalties of race or language, tribe or history which held each one of these men: the Jew and the socialite, the rebel and the downtrodden, the bitter, the defensive and the lost.

Back at St Agnes', the shoots of new life grow. No longer the haven of nostalgia, there is a serious openness to God and his will for the church. The parish is a hive of study and debate about the truth of God and its application. The new arrival and the old stayer are at once engaged in the stimulating search for the right: right worship, right thinking, right doing. Every age group is breaking down barriers, making contacts, reaching out, giving at cost, serving the needy. The brave are supported when risks are taken in sacrifice, protest or lifestyle. The meek are encouraged, the shy put in touch, the chores faithfully covered, the protest made. It was a good day when 300 from Soweto came to worship and stay for lunch for the first time. It was a good day when St Agnes' travelled there to receive hospitality back. It was a good day when every single member wrote to a cabinet minister when Alexandra's curate was detained, and better still to celebrate his release. Now they have to plan the next step of obedience . . .

On the global scene, the debate goes on. The great ecumenical bodies, the denominational offices, the interest-groups from church and mission go on talking. And they must; for although the action is with me and my local church, and these ecumenical debates seem far up in the stratosphere from where we sit, they have access to minds, resources and constituencies which both change the world and fuel the work on the ground. Some questions, however, remain. Are the debaters in touch with the debate? Are the studies all done for God's kingdom? Are the papers and conferences a front for some hidden agenda? Are the channels between world bodies, and between their debate and the church on the ground, in order and operating? Is the spirit of the debaters that of Christ – and is the goal his kingdom?

Love believes the best. Our action needs to secure it, and our words to reflect it. For 'the poor you will always have with you'.

APPENDIX I

Luke, Mark and Matthew

Luke's intentions

Since Luke is the only evangelist to record this incident and its teaching so fully, and to place it in this position in his gospel, it is often asserted that he has created the whole incident, and/or dressed it up, and/or moved it about chronologically, to suit his own theological preoccupation. The whole matter of gospel creation and tradition and the relations between various books is infinitely complex and beyond our scope, yet a few tentative comments are required. Since the main problem is that of Luke's relations to the other 'synoptic' gospels (Matthew and Mark), and since Matthew's account of the outset of Jesus' ministry is fairly similar to Mark's, we can boil this down in two questions –

1. What is the relationship between Luke's account of the launching of Jesus' ministry (Luke 4:13–44) and that of Matthew and Mark (Matthew 4:11–25 and Mark 1:14–39)?
2. What is the relationship between Luke's account of the ministry and conflicts in Nazareth (Luke 4:13–44) and Mark's (Mark 6:1–6) (and less particularly Matthew's in Matthew 13:53–58)?

211

The launching of the ministry

While scholarly disagreements are wide, most thinking
Christians share a certain consensus with the majority of
scholars on a number of basic assumptions. These include,
for example, the assumption that sayings of Jesus and stories
about him, and early collections of both, were in circula-
tion in the early church before any of the gospels came to
be written. Many assume that Matthew and Luke (leaving
aside the special issue of John) had Mark and one or more
other collections before them when they wrote; others
argue that the relationships were the other way round. Most
will grant that the evangelists all exercised a degree of
editorial freedom in the order in which they recorded the
accounts which they had, within certain broad limits; obviously nativity accounts come at the beginning, the passion
accounts at the end, and some key events like the confession
of Peter, the transfiguration of Jesus, and a broad shift from
Galilee towards Judea come somewhere in the middle.
Otherwise events or stories may be clustered according to
theme, place, time or convenience. Sometimes the grouping
principle is obvious, sometimes not; and sometimes the effect
is to highlight one theme or truth above another. Each of the
evangelists appears to throw light on some dimensions of
the gospel more than others, though different readers see
this in different ways. Each evangelist was by definition a
theologian, trying to write meaningful words about God; but
the extent to which each imposed his perspective on his
material is widely debated. Some will be concerned to stress
the enduring core of truth, uninfluenced in itself by whatever sidelights the editor shines; others will almost talk as
if the writers felt free to tell their own story with minimum
concern for historical veracity, marshalling material to back
their individual hobbyhorses. It is within the context of
such a debate that the suspicion arises that Luke is 'up to

something' in the use, order, and maybe adaptation of his material.

It is, thus, argued that Luke inserts into chapter 4 a set of events for which Matthew and Mark do not cater. The argument goes that Jesus appears to begin with a bang in Nazareth, giving his message quite different content to Mark's summary: 'The time has come. The kingdom of God is near. Repent and believe the good news!' (Mark 1:15) or Matthew's, 'Repent, for the kingdom of heaven is near' (Matthew 4:17). Matthew and Mark are alleged to have Jesus set out in Capernaum and to leave any Nazareth ministry until much later.

While I would not need to quarrel with a good case that Luke sets the story here more from 'programmatic significance' than chronological concern, and would count its theological significance undiminished, it is worth noting that the contrast between Luke and Matthew and Mark is easily exaggerated. It is not true that Luke opts for Nazareth against their Capernaum, nor that he plays down the teaching of the kingdom in favour of the reference to Isaiah. Consider what each says in summary:

Matthew's order

1. After the temptation and John's imprisonment, Jesus went to *Galilee* (an area, not a town) (4:12).
2. He left Nazareth (after how long a stay, and after what events?) (4:13).
3. And went to live in Capernaum (4:13).
4. This fulfilled Isaiah 9:1–2 (a different passage, with a different point, from Luke – but the fulfilment of Isaiah in Jesus is in both their words) (4:15–16).
5. Jesus began to preach repentance and the kingdom of heaven (4:17).
6. Jesus called his first disciples (4:18–22).
7. Jesus went all over Galilee teaching, 'preaching the good news of the kingdom' and healing (4:23).

8. News spread to Syria (4:24).
9. Large crowds came from Galilee, Judea, Syria, etc. (4:25).

Mark's order

1. After the temptation and John's imprisonment, Jesus went to Galilee (1:14).
2. There he proclaimed 'the good news of God' (1:14–15).
3. Jesus called the disciples (1:16–20).
4. He went on to Capernaum and caused amazement by his synagogue teaching (1:21–27).
5. News of him spread through Galilee (1:28).
6. Jesus healed Simon Peter's mother-in-law and then many others (1:29–34).
7. After prayer, Jesus decided to move on 'to the nearby villages . . . so I can preach there also' (1:35–38).
8. So he travelled all over Galilee preaching and driving out demons (1:39).

Luke's order

1. After the temptation Jesus returned to Galilee 'in the power of the Spirit', i.e. presumably ministering as well as just travelling (4:14).
2. News of him spread everywhere (4:14).
3. He taught and was praised (4:15).
4. He went to Nazareth and spoke in the synagogue (4:16–30).
5. He then went to Capernaum and taught (4:31–36).
6. News spread again (4:37).
7. Jesus healed Simon's mother-in-law and then many others (4:38–41).
8. After prayer, Jesus decided to move on, saying 'I must preach *the good news of the kingdom of God* to the other towns also' (4:42–43).
9. So he went on to the towns of either Judea, or Galilee, or the 'land of the Jews' (texts vary) (4:44).

In summary, the order of events is really quite close to Matthew and Mark. Matthew implies a visit to Nazareth and Mark does not exclude one; and Luke *does* also speak of preaching about the kingdom of God (4:43). It seems far more likely that Luke saw the exposition of Isaiah 61 as being part of 'the good news of the kingdom', than as an alternative teaching. Granted some narrative licence to the authors, there is no unavoidable inconsistency here – and certainly no more between Luke and the others than between Matthew and Mark.

The visit to Nazareth

It is not only Luke's placing of the Nazareth ministry, but the apparent difference between that ministry and Matthew and Mark's accounts of it, which cause concern. Since Matthew and Mark's accounts are similar and Matthew is most likely to be based on Mark, we simply compare Luke 4 with Mark 6:1–6. As we have examined Luke in detail, here is Mark for comparison:

1. In Mark Jesus has ministered extensively before going to Nazareth, and goes there from the lakeside (probably Capernaum) rather than vice versa.
2. The wording is so similar, while different, that it is hard to see Mark meaning that Jesus had already been to Nazareth with this as a second visit; it must have been the same event.
3. Jesus 'began to teach in the synagogue'; the content of his teaching is not given and, therefore, may well have been that of Luke 4 (some have even suggested that this was anyway his standard 'synagogue sermon').
4. Amazement ensued, with a fuller form of the questions about his family and origins.
5. Offence was taken.

6. Jesus responded with a short form of his words about the prophet's dishonour.
7. An apparently 'softer' ending to the story is given, namely: 'He could not do any miracles there, except lay his hands on a few sick people and heal them. And he was amazed at their lack of faith.'

Here is the main difference: in Mark, Luke's murder attempt is omitted and there is the implication that there was time for *some* ministry to the sick, even if limited. This is a problem, for it really cannot refer to a second visit, at least not after the hostility stirred up in Luke 4. Although we have seen that there is no serious problem in placing Luke's account early in Jesus' ministry, Mark manifestly thinks it was a little later and less drastic in its effects. Granted the compression of so many gospel stories, Luke 4 and Mark 6 *can* be reconciled, but it is hard to avoid the conclusion that either Mark has been a bit vague with the facts, or Luke has painted up the conflict to a sharper pitch than was really the case so very early in the story. Even with the traditional and less hostile translation of Luke 4:23 we have a murder attempt which goes far beyond Mark.

It seems likely, therefore, that Luke has at least 'sited' his story and drawn attention to its conflict elements to indicate just how shocking this message of Jesus was; and this is likely to be for the double reason that he was making religious claims beyond what they could accommodate and that he was implicitly criticising their radical, vengeful, and violent political interpretations of the role of the expected Messiah.

APPENDIX II

The origins of Isaiah 61

'The Lord has anointed me to preach good news to the poor. He has sent me to bind up the broken-hearted, to proclaim freedom for the captives, and release for the prisoners, to proclaim the year of the Lord's favour and the day of vengeance of our God . . .' What did Isaiah think he was preaching?

In view of all we have said about the Old Testament message, there must be both a specific and general answer to that. The specific one will depend upon the point at which we believe this section of Isaiah was written. As we hinted before, there is much dispute about the origins of the present book of Isaiah, and it seems highly likely that at least some of its compilation was completed by followers or admirers of his who were steeped in his thought and vocabulary. The problem arises that we know Isaiah lived in the eighth century BC when the overwhelming political danger to Israel was from the empire of Assyria. This situation is presupposed in Isaiah 1–39. However, Isaiah 40–55 presupposes conditions (and mentions specific names) which can only apply to the exile in Babylon, which (apart from a kind of captive advance party) began in 597 BC. The exile was ended as Cyrus, king of Persia, overthrew the Babylonian empire, so this section announcing his victory is often dated between his first victories in 550 BC and his defeat of Babylon in 538 BC, whereafter he decreed the release of the Jews, to return and reconstruct their land (the histories of Ezra and Nehemiah).

Chapters 56–66 of Isaiah are less of a coherent piece and may contain teaching, prophecies, and odd pieces of material which may be from various periods. The options are, then:

1. That God's Spirit of prophecy gave immense presight as well as insight to the eighth-century Isaiah, who wrote it all.
2. That some at least of the book, which must be composite, was written – or at least edited – during the exile in Babylon in the sixth century.
3. That some of the material may also have been written or finalised at a later date still, after the return from exile, maybe around 520 BC when Haggai and Zechariah were active or even as late as the time of Malachi around the year 450 BC.

For our purposes in understanding Isaiah 61, this means any of five options is possible:

1. If the original eighth-century Isaiah wrote this with his own day in mind (c. 740–700 BC) he could be announcing the goodness of God, which he well knew (Isaiah 4:2–6; 9:1–7) into the oppression in Judah which he was challenging. We shall see that Isaiah ('First Isaiah') was deeply concerned for the poor, and this would have been the reverse side of his message to the rich and powerful, namely that God called them to order their affairs in justice and obedience, feeding the hungry, clothing the naked and cancelling oppression in the land. At the same time, since he was well aware of the spiritual dimensions of Israel's life and the centrality of its worship, it could have been a reaffirmation of the love of God and the need of the people to espouse it. The good news was news of God's love and nearness as well as of his standards and justice. And since 'First Isaiah' was as forward-looking as any prophet, his message would have hinted beyond the

immediate demands of the Lord to the coming day of the servant when these things would be real in a mightier way.

2. If the original Isaiah wrote this by inspiration of the Spirit with Babylon in mind, it would have spoken with special relevance to the brokenhearted, the captives and the prisoners, and an interpolation of the crushed from Isaiah 58:6 would be entirely apposite. His hearers would be breathing the air of Psalm 137, 'By the rivers of Babylon we sat and wept when we remembered Zion.' Isaiah, that is, would be recording promises from God for a situation yet unforeseen by them, a promise which would come into its own in the situation. Neither in the Old Testament nor by comparison with today's experience of New Testament prophecy would such foresight be impossible or unlikely: yet we do not know. What is clear is that both the threat of judgement by exile and the promise of restoration thereafter were given well in advance of the event by Jeremiah, in the latter case seventy years ahead, and quite accurately – so the possibility is wide open.

3. Another prophet of outstanding stature, whose identity has curiously gone unrecorded but who functioned in exile around the mid sixth century BC was given these words of praise in Babylon, for the Jews imprisoned there. The effect of the words would be as at (2), a promise of imminent release from slavery and rejoicing in the return to Zion. 'The poor' would mean – at least in its immediate reference – the exiles.

4. Since Isaiah 56–66 may well have been completed later, a still later prophet may have brought these words in the context of a restored Israel. We know from Haggai that there was a tendency to restore plush homes rather than restore the temple in his day, and this may evidence a similar self-concern as regards the poor and under-privileged. We also know from Malachi that the people of his day, seventy years later, were out of obedience to God

and his Torah, so again a word of God's love and promise to the poor and crushed would be very likely appropriate.

5. Whoever produced it was dominated by the image of the promised servant, and was looking forward to the day of God's great and final liberation, using the experience of exile (for the writer or his people) as the wellspring of vivid meaning out of which to write his ultimate hopes. Remember that the exile was as much a religious and worshipping deprivation as a concrete slavery, and that the hoped-for liberation was as much to do with 'singing the Lord's songs in Zion' as with escaping the jackboot of the Babylonian slave owner. It was inconceivable for a Jew to see liberation or the year of the Lord's favour in solely economic terms, for his fulfilment lay in a fulfilled love and worship of God as much as – if not more than – in material things. That was ever true, so that even the exodus which liberation theology so often borrows as a type of all subsequent social freedom, had a God-centred purpose: that 'you will worship God on this mountain' (Exodus 3:12). Their oppression would form the crucible of eschatological hope.

These are all possible understandings of the literal and circumstantial thrust of Isaiah 61. But there is a broader and more general point which has to be made. As we have seen, the Old Testament speaks to its writers' specific circumstances: yet there is an undertone of common belief which surfaces everywhere. The specifics are rarely really *different*; they are rather different *applications* of a set of underlying central truths. Thus one can trace back most of the law, most of the wisdom literature, and most of the prophets' challenges to a nexus of basic convictions which they are simply teasing out and applying. Every spokesman for God rests his case on the main realities: that God is, and is great, and is love; that man is called to worship and obey him, but has rebelled and gone astray; that individual and social life are to be ordered according to his goodness, with the worship of the one true God at the centre; that this God is active and vocal, calling forth leaders and people to love him, to announce and to do his will. Being great, God will call to account those who wrong him or others, one day doing so gloriously in a crisis of blessing and of judgement.

Without denying the specific applications which any of our options would have *in situ*, would it not be true that in one way the situation does not matter? That in fact Isaiah's 'good news' was simply a chip off the block of the Old Testament's basic assumptions, applied to a cluster of the needs of man? That Old Testament news, announced in various forms and places, seemed good to some and bad to others, depending on their own stance towards it, for the word that judged some freed others? Yet for the poor, be they lost or aimless, hungry or deprived, blind or unjustly in prison, the announcement of God's reality and love would be only good. And in future it would be better still: the programme of Isaiah would be promoted into the priorities of Jesus.

NOTES

Chapter 1

1. The fluctuating exchange rate makes it pointless to try to express the cash value, and anyway people say the pensions vary inexplicably from pay-out to pay-out. But as President Botha puts it, 'South Africa is not a welfare state', and the people who are entitled to a pension at all don't get much.
2. There is dispute over whether to capitalise 'black' and 'white' in print; I haven't.
3. African National Congress; Azanian People's Organisation.
4. An organisation largely peopled by concerned white women and devoted to the welfare of black South Africans.
5. Pastor.
6. Black domestics usually work until after lunch on Sunday.
7. Luke 4:18a.

Chapter 2

1. Luke 4:18–19.
2. Luke 4:14.
3. Luke 4:15.
4. Luke 4:16–21.
5. Luke 4:16.
6. Luke 1:1–4.
7. See, for example, Luke 23:2; Acts 23:23–24:16 and much else.
8. See Acts 17:2, where Luke uses the same phrase of Paul.
9. See Luke 4:15.
10. Luke 4:17.
11. Isaiah 61:1–2.
12. Matthew 5:1–2; John 8:2.

13. Luke 4:21.
14. 1 QH 18:14.
15. 11Q Melchizedek 6–9.
16. M. de Jonge and A. S. van der Woude, '11Q Melchizedek and the New Testament', *New Testament Studies* 12 (1965–66), pp. 301–26.
17. 11Q Melchizedek 16–20; 3–5.
18. Luke 4:24–27.
19. I. Howard Marshall, *The Gospel of Luke: A Commentary on the Greek Text* (Paternoster, 1978), p. 183.
20. Luke 4:18–19.
21. Luke 3:21–22.
22. Genesis 22:2, 12, 16; Psalm 2:7; Isaiah 42:1.
23. Acts 20:25; 28:31; Romans 10:8; Galatians 5:11; 2 Timothy 4:2.
24. e.g. Matthew 26:28; Mark 1:4; Luke 1:77; Acts 2:38; Colossians 1:14; Hebrews 9:22; 10:18, etc.
25. Romans 16:7; Colossians 4:10; Philemon 23.
26. e.g. Isaiah 6:9–10; 42:7.
27. Isaiah 42:6–7.
28. Isaiah 58:6–7.
29. Leviticus 25:4.
30. Leviticus 25:16.
31. The peasant Naboth's reaction to Ahab's attempt to buy his ancestral vineyard reflects the existence of a 'jubilee' attitude to land, and some feel that Ezekiel's 'thirtieth year' was counted from the previous jubilee (Ezekiel 1:1). But the evidence is thin.
32. Amos 5:18–20a, 24.
33. Matthew 16:13–21; Mark 8:27–31; Luke 9:18–22.
34. Mark 8:31.
35. Matthew 16:16.
36. e.g. J. Jeremias and W. Grundmann.

Chapter 3

1. Luke 1:51–52.
2. Exodus 3:7–10.
3. Exodus 18:13–26.
4. Exodus 22:21; 23:9.

5. Mark 12:40.
6. Exodus 22:22.
7. Exodus 22:25–27.
8. Exodus 23:6.
9. Exodus 23:11.
10. Exodus 23:12.
11. Leviticus 19:9–10; 23:22.
12. Leviticus 14:21–22; 12:8; Luke 2:24.
13. Numbers 12:3.
14. Deuteronomy 15:4–5.
15. Deuteronomy 15:7–8.
16. Deuteronomy 15:9.
17. Deuteronomy 15:11.
18. Matthew 26:11.
19. Deuteronomy 24:12–15.
20. Deuteronomy 18:15–19.
21. Exodus 3:1–4:17; 13:1–2; 14:1–4; 19:3–6; 33:7–11; 2 Corinthians 3:7–18.
22. Exodus 2:11f.
23. as promised – Deuteronomy 18:15–19.
24. Judges 6:15.
25. 1 Samuel 18:23.
26. Luke 4:24–27.
27. 2 Samuel 12:1–10.
28. 1 Kings 17:17–24; 21:1–22.
29. 2 Kings 4:38–44.
30. 2 Samuel 12:1–10.
31. 1 Samuel 2:1–10.
32. 1 Samuel 2:8.
33. Luke 2:25.
34. Amos 1:1–2.
35. Amos 7:13.
36. Amos 7:14–15.
37. Amos 8:2.
38. with the exception of *rush*.
39. Amos 1:3–5.
40. Amos 1:6–8.
41. Amos 1:9–10.
42. Amos 1:11–12, cf. v. 6, 9.
43. Amos 1:13–15.

44. Amos 2:1–3.
45. Amos 2:4–5.
46. Amos 2:6–8.
47. Deuteronomy 15:7.
48. See Isaiah 10:1–2.
49. Amos 2:9–11; 3:1–6; 4:6–11; 7:1–9.
50. Amos 2:12; 3:7.
51. Amos 2:13–16; 4:1–3, 12–13; 6:8–14; 8:1–9:10.
52. Amos 3:8–14; 7:10–17; 8:1–3.
53. Amos 4:1.
54. Amos 4:4–5; 5:21–27.
55. Amos 5:1–17.
56. Amos 5:7, 10, 12, 15, 24; 6:12.
57. Amos 5:11.
58. Amos 3:15; 4:1; 5:11; 6:1–7.
59. Amos 5:18–20.
60. Amos 8:4–6.
61. Amos 8:11–12.
62. Amos 9:8.
63. Amos 9:8b–15.
64. Amos 5:24.
65. Isaiah 1:4, 11, 15–17, 23.
66. Isaiah 1:18–20.
67. Isaiah 3:14–15.
68. Isaiah 3:16.
69. Isaiah 10:1–2.
70. Isaiah 10:30.
71. Isaiah 11:1–5.
72. Isaiah 14:30, 32b.
73. Isaiah 25:1, 4–5a.
74. Isaiah 20:1, 5, 6.
75. Isaiah 29:13; cf. 32:7–8.
76. Isaiah 29:19–21.
77. Isaiah 41:17–20.
78. Isaiah 49:13.
79. Isaiah 51:23.
80. Isaiah 51:21–23; 54:11, 13–14.
81. Isaiah 58:6, 7, 10.
82. Isaiah 58:9a.
83. Isaiah 61:4–10.

84. Isaiah 66:2.
85. Zephaniah 3:1; 2:3; 3:10–13.
86. Jeremiah 2:31a, 34.
87. Jeremiah 5:26–29.
88. Jeremiah 20:13.
89. Jeremiah 22:15–17.
90. Ezekiel 16.
91. Ezekiel 18:11b–13a.
92. Ezekiel 18:16.
93. Ezekiel 22:24.
94. Ezekiel 22:25–29.
95. Zechariah 7:9–10 and see verses 11–12.
96. Zechariah 9:9.
97. Zechariah 11:7–11.
98. Zephaniah 3:12.
99. The only way to experience the full impact is to look up the whole:

   anaw: (humble, meek, poor, lowly, afflicted) Psalm 9:12; 10:12, 17; 22:26; 25:9; 34:2; 37:11; 69:32; 76:9; 147:6; 149:4.
   ani: (humble, meek, poor, lowly, afflicted) Psalm 9:17–18; 10:2, 9; 12:5; 14:6; 18:27; 22:24; 25:16; 34:6; 35:10; 37:14; 40:17; 68:10; 69:29; 70:5; 72:2, 4, 12; 74:19; 82:3; 86:1; 88:15; 102:title; 109:16, 22; 140:12.
   ebyon: (desirous, needy, poor – tends to imply material hardship) Psalm 9:18; 12:5; 35:10; 37:14; 40:17; 49:2; 69:33; 70:5; 72:4, 12, 13; 82:4; 86:1; 109:16, 22, 31; 112:9; 113:7; 132:15; 140:12.
   dal: (lean, poor, weak) Psalm 41:1; 72:13; 82:3–4; 113:7.
100. Psalm 9:12, 17–18; 12:5.
101. Psalm 37:10–11.
102. See also Psalm 25:8–9.
103. Psalm 69:30, 32–33a.
104. Psalm 18:27.
105. Psalm 149:4.
106. Psalm 72:1–2, 4, 12–14.
107. Psalm 25:16; 34:6; 40:17; 69:29; 70:5; 86:1.
108. Proverbs 3:34; 16:19.
109. Proverbs 13:23; 14:21; 22:22–23; 29:7; 31:9.
110. Proverbs 31:20.
111. Proverbs 28:3, 15; 29:14.

112. Proverbs 14:31.
113. Proverbs 30:7–9.
114. Job 24:1, 4, 9, 14.
115. Job 36:5–6.
116. Job 29:11–12.
117. Job 36:13–15.
118. Ecclesiastes 5:8.
119. Acts 16:7; Philippians 1:19.
120. John 7:39.
121. Genesis 8:1; 2:7; Judges 3:10.
122. Genesis 2:7.
123. Exodus 15:8–10; Isaiah 40:7.
124. Exodus 31:3; 35:31 and possibly 28:3.
125. 1 Samuel 16:14–16; 1 Kings 22:19–23; 1 Samuel 9:9, 18, 19; 11:6; 19:20–24; 2 Kings 2:9, 15; Isaiah 61:1.
126. Numbers 11:17; Deuteronomy 34:9; 1 Samuel 16:13.
127. See Psalm 89:20 for the relationship.
128. 1 Kings 22:5–28; Isaiah 28:7; Jeremiah 6:13; 23:9–40; Amos 7:10–17.
129. Jeremiah 15:17; 20:9, etc.
130. Isaiah 59:21.
131. See Ezekiel 2:2; 3:1–4; 22:24.
132. Psalm 53.
133. Isaiah 63:10.
134. Psalm 143:10.
135. As in Isaiah 61 and beautifully in 4:4 and 11:2.
136. Ezekiel 36:26; Jeremiah 31:31–34.
137. Isaiah 32:15; 44:3; Ezekiel 39:29; Joel 2:28; Zechariah 12:10.
138. Isaiah 42, 61.

Chapter 4

1. Luke 1:19.
2. Luke 2:25–38.
3. Luke 1:17; 2:10–11.
4. Luke 1:1–4.
5. Luke 2:24 cf. Leviticus 12:6–8.
6. Luke 2:25–38.
7. Luke 1:6.

8. Luke 1:13.
9. Luke 1:41–45.
10. Luke 1:67–79.
11. Luke 1:38.
12. Luke 2:22, 41.
13. Luke 2:25–28.
14. Luke 2:36–38.
15. Luke 1:46–55.
16. Luke 3:18.
17. Luke 3:3.
18. Luke 3:8.
19. Luke 3:10–14.
20. Luke 3:21–23.
21. Luke 4:2.
22. Luke 4:8.
23. Luke 4:18–19.
24. Luke 4:14–15.
25. Luke 4:36.
26. Luke 4:44.
27. Luke 5:1.
28. Luke 5:4.
29. Luke 5:6, 10–11.
30. Luke 5:8.
31. Luke 5:17.
32. Luke 5:26.
33. Luke 5:33–39.
34. Luke 6:1–5.
35. Luke 6:6–11.
36. Luke 6:17–49.
37. Luke 6:17–19; 7:1.
38. Luke 7:1–10.
39. Luke 7:11–16.
40. Luke 7:17.
41. Luke 7:18–23.
42. Luke 7:24–28.
43. Luke 7:29–35.
44. Luke 7:41–43.
45. Luke 7:44–47.
46. Luke 8:1–3.
47. Luke 8:4–15.

48. Luke 8:19–21.
49. Luke 8:22–25.
50. Luke 8:37.
51. Luke 8:26–39.
52. Luke 8:51–56.
53. Luke 9:1–9.
54. Luke 10:1–20.
55. Luke 10:15.
56. Luke 9:10–17.
57. Luke 9:18–27.
58. Luke 9:28–36.
59. Luke 9:23.
60. Luke 9:46–50.
61. Luke 9:57–62.
62. Luke 10:25–37.
63. Luke 10:38–42.
64. Luke 11:1–13.
65. Luke 11:14–28.
66. Luke 11:27–28.
67. Luke 11:37–54.
68. Luke 12:1–12.
69. Luke 12:13–21.
70. Luke 12:22–59.
71. Luke 13.
72. Luke 14.
73. Luke 15.
74. Luke 16:1–18.
75. Luke 16:19–31.
76. Luke 18:18–27.
77. Luke 18:9–14.
78. Luke 18:35–43.
79. Luke 19:1–10.
80. Luke 19:28–44.
81. Luke 20:1.
82. Luke 21:5–38.
83. Luke 22.
84. Luke 24:27.
85. Luke 24:32.
86. Luke 24:45.
87. Acts 1:3.

88. Luke 4:38–39.
89. See my *Who Cares?*, Lakeland 1979, p. 10, 17f.
90. Luke 4:40–41.
91. Luke 4:42–44.
92. Luke 5:12–16.
93. Luke 5:13.
94. Luke 5:17–26.
95. Luke 6:6–11.
96. Luke 11:46.
97. Luke 9:1.
98. in Luke 6:17.
99. Luke 6:19.
100. Luke 7:1–10.
101. Luke 7:11–17.
102. Luke 7:18–23.
103. Luke 8:40–56.
104. Luke 8:46.
105. Luke 9:11.
106. Luke 10:9; cf. 11:20.
107. Luke 13:10–17 and 14:1–6.
108. Luke 13:16.
109. Luke 17:11–19.
110. Luke 18:35–43.
111. Mark 10:52; Acts 9:2; 22:4; etc.
112. Luke 13:14, 16.
113. Luke 4:40–41; 6:17–19. (The passing reference to Mary Magdalene in 8:1–3 may suggest either distinction or overlap, depending upon how one reads the list of names.)
114. Luke 9:37–43.
115. Mark 9:14–29.
116. Luke 11:14.
117. Luke 4:31–37.
118. Luke 8:26–39.
119. Luke 11:24–26, which tells what happens otherwise.
120. Mark 1:35–39.
121. Luke 5:1–11.
122. Luke 5:27–32.
123. Luke 6:12; cf. 6:17; 7:1.
124. Luke 6:27.
125. Luke 6:27–49.

126. Luke 8:9–10.
127. Luke 8:16–18.
128. Luke 8:22–25.
129. Luke 8:36.
130. Luke 9:1–6, 10.
131. Luke 9:1–17.
132. Luke 9:18–27.
133. Luke 8:51–55.
134. Luke 9:28–36.
135. Luke 9:46–50.
136. Luke 10:1–24.
137. Luke 9:18.
138. Luke 11:1–13.
139. Luke 12:1.
140. Luke 12:2–34.
141. Luke 12:41.
142. Luke 12:54.
143. Luke 14:15–24.
144. Luke 14:25–35.
145. Luke 5:27–29.
146. Luke 17:1–10.
147. Luke 17:20–37.
148. Luke 18:1–8.
149. Luke 18:31–34.
150. Luke 19:29–36; 22:7–38.
151. Luke 21:5–36.
152. Luke 21:37–38.
153. John 13:1.
154. Luke 22; cf. John 13.
155. Luke 22:48.
156. Luke 22:61.
157. Luke 24.
158. Luke 5:17–26.
159. Luke 5:27–32.
160. Luke 7:36–50.
161. Luke 14:15–24.
162. Luke 19:1–10.
163. Luke 19:10.
164. Matthew 26:28.
165. Luke 24:46f.

166. Luke 5:27–32.
167. Luke 19:1–10.
168. Luke 3:12–14.
169. Luke 16:19–31.
170. Leviticus 19:18.
171. Luke 11:42.
172. Luke 11:46.
173. Luke 13:31–32; 23:7–12.
174. Luke 20:47.
175. Luke 19:45–48f; Jeremiah 7:1–11.
176. Jeremiah 7:5–6.
177. Luke 22:52.
178. Luke 16:13–14.
179. Luke 7:36; 11:37; 14:1.
180. Luke 11:37–54.
181. Luke 14:7–14.
182. Luke 12:13–21.
183. Luke 14:15–24.
184. Luke 14:25–35.
185. Luke 18:18–30.
186. Luke 21:1–4.
187. Luke 6:20–26.
188. Luke 16:1–9.
189. Luke 16:10–12.
190. Luke 6:30–38.
191. Luke 12:33.
192. Luke 4:4.
193. Matthew 15:32.
194. Mark 6:34.
195. Mark 8:2.
196. John 6.
197. Luke 9:10–17.
198. Luke 6:21.
199. Luke 7:11–17.
200. Luke 23:27–31.
201. Luke 24:13–49.
202. Luke 6:22.
203. Luke 21:12–19.
204. Luke 12:11–12.
205. Luke 10:38–42.

206. Luke 12:22–34.
207. Luke 21:5–36.
208. Luke 8:1–3.
209. Luke 2:51 and 8:19.
210. Luke 8:40–56.
211. Luke 13:10–13.
212. Luke 24:1–11.
213. Luke 20:27–40.
214. Luke 18:15–17.
215. Luke 9:46–48.
216. Luke 7:2, 9.
217. Luke 8:26–39.
218. Luke 11:29–32.
219. Luke 14:16–24.
220. Psalm 23.
221. Luke 20:9–16.
222. Luke 24:47.
223. John 4:3–4.
224. John 4:5–26, 28–30, 39–42.
225. Luke 9:51–56.
226. Luke 10:25–37.
227. Luke 17:11–19.
228. Acts 1:8.

Chapter 5

1. Luke 6:17–26.
2. Luke 5:33–39.
3. Luke 6:1–11.
4. Luke 6:12–16.
5. Matthew 5:3, NEB – rather unusually for its translators.
6. J. R. W. Stott, *Christian Mission in the Modern World* (Falcon Press, 1975), p. 92. This is quite a step on from his own, otherwise classic, exposition in *Christian Counter-culture* (IVP, 1978), p. 30ff.
7. Matthew 6:5.
8. John 15:18–25.
9. Luke 6:27–45.

10. Luke 6:46–49.
11. Luke 9:23–27.
12. Luke 9:57–62.
13. Luke 10:1–24.
14. Luke 11:1–13.
15. Luke 11:14–23, 33–36.
16. Luke 12:1.
17. Luke 12:3.
18. Luke 12:4–12.
19. Luke 11:13; 12:10.
20. Luke 12:22–34.
21. Luke 12:31, 34.
22. Luke 12:33.
23. Luke 12:35–59.
24. Luke 14:12–14.
25. Luke 17:1–4.
26. Luke 17:5–6.
27. Luke 17:7–10.
28. Luke 17:9–10; 14:7–11.
29. Luke 17:20–37.
30. Luke chapters 22, 24.
31. Luke 24:45–53.
32. Matthew 20:1–16.
33. Luke 15.
34. Luke 11:5–10.
35. Luke 18:1–8.
36. Luke 7:41–43.
37. Luke 8:1–15.
38. Luke 13:19, 20.
39. Luke 6:46–49.
40. Luke 8:8.
41. Luke 13:24.
42. Luke 14:15–24.
43. Luke 14:28, 31.
44. Luke 15:11–32.
45. Luke 18:9–14.
46. Luke 6:43–45.
47. Luke 6:46–49.
48. Luke 8:16–17.
49. Luke 11:21–26.

50. Luke 12:35–40; 14:21–24; 15:22–24; 16:1–13; 17:7–10; 19:11–27.
51. Luke 6:46–49.
52. Luke 18:9.
53. Luke 19:11–27 especially 20–23.
54. Luke 20:9–19.
55. Luke 6:46–49.
56. Luke 8:14.
57. Luke 12:13–21.
58. Luke 14:18–20.
59. Luke 15:13.
60. Luke 16:19–31.
61. Luke 7:39–47.
62. Luke 10:30–35; 14:23.
63. Luke 15.
64. Luke 16:19–31.
65. Luke 14:12–14.
66. Matthew 25:31–46.
67. Luke 12:35–48.
68. Luke 6:49.
69. Luke 13:6–9.
70. Luke 14:24.
71. Luke 13:25, 27.
72. Luke 16:24.
73. Luke 19:24.
74. Luke 20:16.

Chapter 6

1. Acts 1:1.
2. Acts 1:8.
3. 1 Peter 3:15.
4. Acts 2:14–36.
5. Acts 3:1–10; 4:16.
6. Acts 4:10.
7. Acts 4:1–4.
8. Acts 4:5–22.
9. Acts 5:12–16.

10. Acts 6:1–7.
11. Acts 8:1–25.
12. Acts 9:1–30.
13. Acts 9:36.
14. Acts 10:36.
15. Acts 10:42–43.
16. Acts 11:20.
17. Acts 11:27–30.
18. Galatians 2:10.

Chapter 7

1. G. Gutierrez, *A Theology of Liberation* (SCM, 1974), quoted in J. Andrew Kirk, *Liberation Theology: An Evangelical View from the Third World* (Marshall, Morgan and Scott, 1979), p. 23.
2. See Kirk's critique of their use of the exodus motif, *Liberation Theology*, chapter 8, 'A Privileged Text: The Exodus' and chapter 14, 'Why the Exodus? Which Exodus?'
3. David Sheppard, *Built as a City* (Hodder and Stoughton, 1974) and *Bias to the Poor* (Hodder and Stoughton, 1983).
4. *Bias*, p. 113.
5. ibid., p. 151.
6. ibid., p. 91.
7. ibid., pp. 221, 155.
8. ibid., p. 201.
9. Quoted in Professor David Bosch's review of Melbourne, 'In search of mission: reflections on "Melbourne" and "Pattaya" ' in *Missionalia*, the journal of the South African Missiological Society, 9/1 (1981), p. 9.
10. Metropolitan Anthony, 'On Mission and Evangelism', *International Review of Mission*, 276–7 (October 1980–January 1981), pp. 477–80; the quotation occurs on p. 479.
11. In its original form it can be found in *Missionalia*, 9/1, above.
12. The Lausanne Covenant, from section 5c.
13. J. R. W. Stott, *Christian Mission in the Modern World* (Falcon Press, 1975).
14. ibid., p. 15.
15. ibid., p. 23.

16. ibid., p. 27.
17. ibid., p. 19.
18. ibid., p. 18.
19. ibid., p. 48.
20. J. R. W. Stott, *Issues Facing Christians Today* (Marshalls, 1984).
21. ibid., p. 14.
22. For one illustration of how these issues have exercised the minds of Christians committed to mission in the past, see the new biography of Henry Venn, who was responsible for the work of the Church Missionary Society for much of the nineteenth century: Wilbert R. Schenk, *Henry Venn – Missionary Statesman* (Orbis Books, 1983).
23. *Missionalia* 10/2 (1982), pp. 78–88.
24. Desmond Mpilo Tutu, *Hope and Suffering: Sermons and Speeches* (Skotoville Publishers, Johannesburg, 1983), pp. 58–59.

Chapter 8

1. John 8:28–29.
2. Romans 8:11.
3. Says the Rev. Dave Dargie, Roman Catholic musical expert in Southern Africa.
4. Ephesians 4:16.
5. Revelation 5:9–10.
6. Colossians 1:28.
7. See, for example, Howard Snyder, *New Wineskins* (Marshall, Morgan and Scott, 1977) or David Prior, *The Church in the Home* (Marshall, Morgan and Scott, 1983).
8. James 1:22.
9. Published as *Faith for the Fearful?* Diakonia, Durban, 1984.
10. I am indebted to my friend Dr Michael Schluter, co-founder of the Jubilee Centre for the study of the relevance of Old Testament legislation to modern social policy, for much material in this section. His address is:

    The Jubilee Centre,
    19A Sturton Street,
    Cambridge, CB1 2QB.
11. *Family Policy in Old Testament Israel: some lessons for British social policy in the 1980s*, M. Schluter and R. Clements, May 1983.

12. Schluter and Clements.
13. Matthew 28:19; Mark 16:15; Luke 24:48; John 20:21; Acts 1:8.
14. Acts 2:23.
15. Isaiah 53:7–8, quoted in Acts 8:32; Isaiah 53:6.
16. Acts 2:38.